Relax, Breathe, Feel

Three Keys Toward Mastery of Life in the World

BILL NIELSEN

Copyright 2010 Bill Nielsen

ISBN 978-0-557-55139-2

About This Book

This book does not have a beginning, middle, and an end. This book has 100 titles. They wouldn't all fit on the cover, so they are contained within. You needn't read them all, though it is my hope that you will find each worthy of your attention. On any given day, find a title (or two) that intrigues you and give it a whirl, then sit with it awhile.

Regarding reading in general, I agree with Richard Bach, of *Jonathan Livingston Seagull* fame. In the vast majority of books we find ourselves like great baleen whales, taking in huge seawater mouthfuls of information and then strain out the few nuggets of real nourishment contained within them. I'm not saying it isn't worth the trouble. It's just that offering just nuggets might save you a lot of time.

Acknowledgements

I would first like to offer my thanks to Steven and Lia Ridley of Denver, CO. Thank you Steve, for your enthusiastic support, skillful editing, and many helpful suggestions in bringing this work to fruition, and thank you Lia, for the beautiful cover photo of Steve. Thanks to my son, Caleb, for your computer work on the cover. My thanks as well to my friends Dusanka Mitchell, Andrea Alton, and Barry Ryan for their reading of early drafts and taking the time to discuss and offer constructive criticism of the ideas expressed.

I would also like to offer my sincere gratitude to my wife, dear friend, and beautiful partner, Cori; for the long hours at the computer, typing, editing, and making sense of my often unintelligible scribblings; for your patience in dealing with the seemingly endless changes to the first drafts; and most importantly, for remaining steadfast through difficult times, and opening my heart to the healing power of Love. Without you, there would be no book.

A List of Titles

1. A New Beginning 1
2. A Bit of Personal History 4
3. Getting Comfortable 6
4. It's About Balance 8
5. Be Still and Know 9
6. It's All in How You See It 10
7. What Dreams May Come 11
8. What You See Is What You Get 13
9. Enlightenment - Not As Rare As You Think 14
10. The Zombies Want YOU! 16
11. It's Different Every Time 17
12. Be the Big Hermit 19
13. A Deep Reverence for Life 21
14. The Path to Real Power 22
15. It's Not Supposed to Make You Crazy 23
16. Cease to Cherish Opinions 25
17. We Are One 26
18. Breathe! 27
19. Negative Energy 28
20. Rest 29
21. Never-Ending Creation 30
22. What Is Enlightenment? 31
23. Who Was Jesus Really? 32
24. The Big Picture 34
25. War and Peace 37
26. Home Sweet Home 39

27.	Let Life Jump on You!	44
28.	On the Road to Enlightenment	45
29.	Peace and Quiet	47
30.	It's Not What You Think	49
31.	A History Lesson	52
32.	Self Inquiry	54
33.	A Mayan View of Time	56
34.	From Rudolph Steiner's	59
35.	Anchor Deep	60
36.	Some Days You're the Pigeon, Some Days the Statue	61
37.	Lighten Up	62
38.	In Gratitude	64
39.	Short and Sweet	65
40.	A Koan	66
41.	Simplicity	67
42.	On Righteousness	68
43.	The Subtlety of Words	69
44.	The Cathedral of Mind	70
45.	Safe Harbor	72
46.	I Am Not a Buddhist	73
47.	The Many Ways of Knowing	74
48.	Know What's Gotta Go	76
49.	Just Another Day in Paradise	78
50.	Let's be Honest	79
51.	Open and Allow	81
52.	Awakening Your Subtle Senses	83
53.	On Seekers	85
54.	Dreaming The Ego's Dream	87
55.	A Day on the Hill	89
56.	Know Thyself	91

57.	On Fitness	94
58.	The Heart Has its Reasons	96
59.	This Is Relating?	97
60.	Save The Earth?	98
61.	In Search of Truth	100
62.	The Enigma of Knowing Nothing	103
63.	The Dragon's Path.	105
64.	The Circle of Life	106
65.	Mind	108
66.	A Little One on One with Source	109
67.	On Climbing	111
68.	The Occasional Apocalypse	113
69.	High School Days	116
70.	It's All About Patterns	118
71.	Love Is!	120
72.	The Downside of Belief	121
73.	It's Not Personal	123
74.	Bad Connections	125
75.	Negativity is Contagious	127
76.	On Irritation	129
77.	Through The Back Door	131
78.	Freedom - It's Closer than You Think	134
79.	Ride the Wave	136
80.	The Recognition of Innocence	138
81.	Open Heart, Open Mind	140
82.	Are You a Piano in a Marching Band?	142
83.	The Shining	144
84.	Old Solomon Was Mistaken	146
85.	Nature Always Wins	147
86.	All Hail Bread and Circuses!	149

87.	Quantum Weirdness	151
88.	Skin to Skin, Heart to Heart	153
89.	It is what it is	155
90.	Synchronicity	157
91.	Attention!	159
92.	The Mission	161
93.	It Is, and It Is Not	163
94.	Ten Steps To a Better You	164
95.	Life Is a Trickster	165
96.	Holy Fire	166
97.	Coincidentia Oppositorum	168
98.	It Takes a Warrior's Spirit	170
99.	Is It God, or Is It You?	172
100.	Choose Wisely and Well	174

Introduction

I've just recently returned from a fine adventure. A few months back, a dear friend shared with me his desire to relocate to California. At the time, we both lived in the South suburbs of Chicago. Now I do, and he does not. He answered his heart's call and now resides in Escalon, California with his wife and three children. He is one of those rare individuals that trust life. I helped him move. We packed all his worldly goods into a truck, and a van, and a trailer and hauled it across the country, just the two of us.

The lure to which I responded in throwing in with him was an opportunity to venture through the great American West, and his promise that upon reaching our destination he would take me to the one place in the world he feels closest to God, the great Yosemite Valley in Yosemite National Park.

Truck, trailer, and van unloaded, true to his word, we ventured off together yet again, to his beloved valley. A place so magnificent words fail me. A place of monolithic pines nestled between towering granite bluffs, and more waterfalls than I'd seen in my whole life, all in a single 13 mile long valley - God's living room to be sure.

Seven months into my 60th journey around the sun, I took a little hike with my friend Justin to the top of Yosemite Falls. Though some 24 years my junior, our friendship seemed to be founded on pushing each other's limits. And this was to be no exception. The trail rose over 2,500 feet from the valley floor in just 3.4 miles. I'll not be forgetting that little stroll anytime soon. More than a few fellow adventurers fell by the way, and turned back down the trail before reaching the top. Some underestimated what was required and didn't bring enough water. Some overestimated their ability and charged recklessly up the slope (mostly the young) to be discovered further on, by the side of the path, pale and prostrated in great distress. Slow and steady I made my way, resting often, breathing deeply. Each step becoming a meditation in forbearance.

The view from the top into the valley below was glorious! The pools of cool water in the stream rushing headlong to the precipice were refreshing and clear. Their currents and eddies soothing my wobbly legs as I waded through them, sipping handfuls along the way. Taking it all in, I felt full, content, utterly connected to the heart of something beyond my comprehension, and yet, somehow familiar.

The very fact that I'd made it to the top seemed a minor miracle. On my way down I kept my aching feet from overwhelming my otherwise thoroughly enjoyable experience by trying to recall other times in my life that I'd been so physically tested. The only thing I could come up with that even came close, was a 50 mile forced march in basic training back in 1969. I was 20.

Here I am, 40 years later and I stand in awe at the powers of this incredible self-sustaining energy matrix that is my body, and its herculean capacities that carry me so efficiently through the realms of space and time. I must also admit to a deep and abiding gratitude that was born when Qigong practice completely healed my torn and tattered knee back in 1986. It continues to contribute to the physical health; emotional stability; incisive mental functioning, and the constant awareness of the realm of spirit that permeates my life in each and every moment.

All that has come to me through my practice, I wish for you. It is why I am committed to sharing it with any and all that wish to learn, for as long as I live. I write to let you know how it changes things. This isn't another book on the How of Qigong. There are plenty of those. It's more about the Why of it. It is my sincere wish that you find your time among these pages well spent.

I love Tai Chi Qigong. It has opened and healed me in ways I could never have forseen. It can likely do the same for you. All that I share within, you can know as the truth, if that is your intent.

Many years ago I spent a wonderful evening with Dr. Gay Luce, at the time, the only American, female ordained Buddhist monk I had ever encountered. She was in the Chicago area to promote the newly founded Nine Gates Program, an eclectic mix of many of the great mystical schools from around the world.

Two things followed me home that evening. The first was, that we can love (or more accurately be in Love with) someone for a moment, an hour, an evening, and it will be as powerful and true as any long-term love we will ever know. Love's duration in time has nothing to do with its authenticity or its power.

The second was a statement she made regarding why we should embrace and practice every day, one of the ancient ways of knowing: "Without a daily practice," she said, "we tend to get small."

If there is any battle worth fighting, it is that. It is a battle waged almost universally, every single day, in the hearts of the best of men, and women, I have come to love in this life. They all refuse to be small. I would go so far as to say that it is the one quality in others that spontaneously evokes my deepest respect and admiration. Life as a human being is complicated. We are so multifaceted. We live our lives simultaneously on so many levels at once. There's the world, and then our experience of the world, colored by countless emotions, born of memories, dreams and reflections of what could have, would have, should have been. Countless interpretations come together at lightning speed, in our hearts and minds. Finding a pattern that will make it all mean something is what we do. How many times every day do we tirelessly stumble through this tangle, getting caught, falling down, fighting our way to our feet again, cursing or praising, our luck, or God, or life itself?

How enduring we are. Yet, just enduring won't change anything. If we are to become fully human, we must be brave in the face of whatever adversity comes our way. We must be bold, unafraid to face life's challenges head-on. We are not fate's hapless victims. If we would live this life to the full we must sincerely try, with every fiber of our being, to master this experience of 'humanness'.

It is not a hopeless situation. We just tend to get stuck from time to time in this wild and unpredictable terrain that we're literally forced by life to negotiate. We're all just muddling our way through, trying to find some meaning, to see some pattern in it all. Life on planet Earth is *all* about patterns. The trick is to see them before we become trapped by them. As my Dear friend and teacher Steven would say, "Patterns can be useful, contributing to order and function, but needn't be over-identified with."

Sometimes we get stuck just for a moment, if we have become skilled at finding our way through it all. Sometimes we get stuck longer

– much, much, longer. It's not personal. It is what we are subject to - being human.

Being human is like learning to drive. To properly operate the vehicle certain skills are required. It isn't just physical. There are rules to be followed and understood. One must learn to focus attention, to balance emotional influences. Know where you are, where you're headed, and when you've arrived. A good teacher certainly helps, and then - practice, practice, practice – attentively open to discovery while refining applications.

Whether it is driving a car, or living a life, the more you practice the more skilled you become. With vigilance, accidents will happen a little less often, but know they WILL happen. With practice, you'll break free into the clear seeing of the how and why of it a little faster each time. It is the subtle yearning for *that* kind of freedom that tugs at every human heart. With a little luck and a touch of grace, each of us can transcend the habitual patterns of our lives and begin to awaken to the pull of our heart's deepest desire, and then dedicate ourselves, with a warrior's resolve, to follow it relentlessly to its source.

1.

A New Beginning

When I first came to Qigong it was because I was hurt, for the first time in my life. I was living in Bemidji, MN, at the time. I'd torn up my right knee in a twisting fall. There were no broken bones, but all of those interesting little ligaments and tendons holding my kneecap in place were pretty much trashed. The ER doctor said that without an operation I'd probably walk with a cane for the rest of my life. I was 36 years old, self-employed, the father of three boys, with no insurance, and this guy was telling me I was going to walk with a limp for the rest of my life. He scared the hell out of me.

I was still on painkillers and wearing a brace when my nine year old son brought me a martial arts magazine one of his friends had loaned him so he could show me a knife he really liked. The "Super Slasher III", as I recall. After a brief discussion, the gist of which was "No Way!" he sulked off leaving me with the magazine. As I thumbed through it I came across an advertisement. "Harness the Ancient Healing Power of Qigong," it said.

I was intrigued. The following day a friend drove me into town. I hobbled through the local used bookstore and found a doorstop sized volume with 280 easy to follow photos of master someone or other and started a brisk slide into a funk. (Funks were a pretty common occurrence in those days). It became immediately evident that this was not something I was going to learn from a book. As I was leaving I could tell that the owner who had led me to the book was disappointed that I was leaving empty-handed. When I shared my realization that I didn't think Tai Chi was going to be something a book could teach me he said, "Well if it's a teacher you're looking for, there's a lady in the office building around the corner that offers classes. I've seen them practicing down by the lake." The Gods had smiled on me.

Her name was Jeanne Carlson. She changed my life. She taught me Justin Stone's Tai Chi Chih. It consists of 19 movements and a standing pose. I learned the first ten movements in my first session. I practiced twice a day, every day. I learned the rest of the movements a week later.

Each time I practiced it felt like my knee was on fire. On the other hand, it was a novelty compared to the incessant dull ache I was used to. At least something new was happening. Tai Chi Chih was so gentle I was confident I wasn't hurting myself. Things began to get better – fast. I began to think I might be as good as new if I just kept it up, and that's just what happened.

As I continued to heal and work on mastering the form, Jeanne started encouraging me to go with her to a teacher's training. After months of hearing her say I'd make a good teacher, I started to believe her. The plan started to unfold. This was no small thing. Perhaps a little background is in order.

Bemidji, Minnesota was not always home sweet home. I'm from the south side of Chicago. Just about the time I would have been sucked into the whole street gang thing, my family joined the white flight to the South Chicago suburbs. That was home for most of my life. Still is.

My father was a railroader, as his father was, as I was. That is until Uncle Sam had a better idea and a little all expenses paid trip to Southeast Asia eventually ensued. Just like Forest Gump, life picked me up and swept me along.

The one good thing that came from that dirty little war was meeting the best friend of my life. Dave was Minnesota born and bred. The call of the North woods pulled on him the same way it eventually pulled on me.

After serving our time, we visited every year, and after he moved from St. Paul to Bemidji I started visiting him there. With each visit, when the time came to leave, my heart grew heavier and heavier until I could bear it no longer. I quit my railroad job of 17 years and moved to Bemidji in the fall of '83 with my wife and three boys who were 6, 4, and 18 Months.

We lived in a trailer in the woods. I spent my days working with my friend, printing T-shirts, making signs, walking up my driveway to go to work at his house. It felt like heaven. Two years later I was hurt, broke, and my marriage was starting to crumble.

So you see, when Qigong came into my life, it was darn close to a miracle. From that time, the miracles have continued fast and hard. One of the things I've learned from Qigong practice is that when we open up to an ever expanding vision of life, little miracles become commonplace. You just have to keep your mind and heart open enough to see them. Life's most precious gifts come to us through grace. Whatever you find that opens you to that grace, hold it dear. It is the breadth of your vision, expanding or contracting, that ultimately determines your reality.

2.

A Bit of Personal History

There are those daily practices (I almost said disciplines, but that's such a scary word) which are quite rigid in terms of their proper execution. There are also those that are a mix and match affair of various traditions, Qigong lies somewhere in the middle. It's quite simple for the most part, and yet marvelously profound in its effects. In my life I have been a practicing Catholic, an Evangelical Christian, an agnostic, a student of hatha yoga, a student of Zen Buddhism, a practitioner of Transcendental Meditation, and a shirt-tail Taoist with a deep respect for the Native American traditions.

There was also a stint as an atheist which gradually evolved into my becoming a devoted student of *A Course in Miracles*. Which in retrospect, seemed to be an attempt to re-order things in a way devoid of prior religious influences. It wasn't as if I no longer believed in God. I was just no longer sure of what exactly God was.

I'll never forget how profoundly Henry David Thoreau's *Walden* influenced my young mind. Like the Taoist sages of old, how powerfully nature spoke to him. I also loved his incisive wit. Even on his death bed when asked if he'd made his peace with God, he softly replied, "I wasn't aware that God and I had quarreled." I also deeply enjoy the wisdom of Gautama the Buddha; Teilhard de Chardin, Jesus the Christ, Paramahansa Yogananda, Sri Aurobindo, Osho (Bhagwan Shree Rajneesh), Eckhart Tolle and Yogi Berra (especially Yogi Berra, he's *so* Zen. When someone yelled out to him in the locker room one day, "Hey Yogi, what time is it?" he replied, "You mean NOW?")

Truth opens you wherever you find it. That is its calling card. It doesn't really work for me to identify with this and not that anymore. When your vision expands, so does what you are. Despite what you may have read, or heard, a deep desire to keep opening and growing is required to sustain the effort.

For more than a few years I defined myself as an ecumenical eclectic when it came to matters of faith. If there is a definition of what I have become I haven't thought of it, or found it, but then I haven't been looking. I just practice and teach Qigong. For me, that is enough. Transcending perceived limitations is my chief intention these days, and for that Qigong serves very well.

3.

Getting Comfortable

I love books. I like how they look. I like how they feel. Most of the time, I like how they smell. I don't have a strong connection to works of fiction. I like non-fiction, seeing the world through another's eyes, sharing their thoughts, listening to their experiences. Share with me what you know, how you came to know it, why you think it's true. I want to know all of it. To what end? Why to be a "know it all" of course! (And I was a real chatterbox for a time. Thank you friends and family for suffering through that).

I love how truth refuses to be pinned down. The universe is expanding. There will be a bunch of stuff here tomorrow that wasn't here today, and every discovered answer just creates another question ad infinitum. So… to get comfortable with not knowing is a reasonable course of action, don't you think?

Easy to say, hard to do. Getting comfortable with being uncomfortable makes me sound like I'm out of my mind. To accomplish it, it turns out that's exactly what is required. When things don't make any sense, don't despair, it's a sign you're on the right track. When the old reference point isn't holding center, a new center is moving into place. Let it.

One of my favorite sayings of Paramahansa Yogananda is "Center everywhere, circumference nowhere." As I mentioned, it thrills me to the core when someone gets the words just right. I never tire of my heart's sweet embrace of a truth well-spoken, the melting warmth that surges softly through me upon the reading of a simple phrase perfectly expressing the ineffable.

But getting back to being comfortable… I'm writing in my favorite bookstore, having a cup of my favorite coffee. I just finished teaching a class and I'm as comfy and snug as a bug in a rug. Yet comfort, like having a momentary hold on truth, is a fleeting thing. I know, as soon as I start moving in the world outside of my cloister cafe, ten thousand things will begin clamoring for my attention - so much for ease and comfort. I am challenged to move, relax & breathe, in the midst of it all, to f-e-e-l life moving, to move with it.

The key is to relax. Let go of all tension. Don't give unwarranted fear or apprehension a place in you to hold on to. B-r-e-a-t-h-e. Tension is the glue that knots your internal energy, creating an internal state that will reflect (and spontaneously recreate) the fear and apprehension that put it there. Whenever your breath stops you are reflecting past pain, and at the same time, insuring future suffering in an endless cycle. Stop it! You have the power to shift your perspective. Skillfully relax and breathe.

Life Rule #1 – Keep Breathing. This lies at the heart of all practice.

4.

It's About Balance

Many years ago, shortly after returning from my government sponsored trip to Southeast Asia, I read a book that had a profound effect upon my life. It was *Be Here Now* by Ram Dass, formerly Dr. Richard Alpert. I was a bit of a high-head in those days. Yet I was not so much a partier as someone trying to find the shortest route to Nirvana. (Feel free to use that one when necessary.)

I remember very vividly an analogy in that wildly creative exposition, of a great big ice cream cone. How the mind always goes for the "more is better" approach to satisfying our desires. The natural result of which is a great big belly ache.

I used to call it "the promise of one thing". You know, the one thing that will bring all your suffering to an end; that perfect job, trip, house, car, or relationship that triggers that wonderful "And then I'll live happily ever after" state of mind. I don't beat myself up anymore for all the energy I wasted on that one. You shouldn't either.

More isn't better. Balance is better. But balance is such a subtle thing. How do you know when you're there? Most often you just know when you're not. "Ouch!" being the most common indicator.

Finding out where center lies is the first step toward balance. Pretty soon you begin to sense when you're balanced and when you're not, moving through life from a constant center, greeting life from a state of inner knowing that all is well. Life just happens, and it doesn't have to hurt. It takes a bit of time and practice, but it's *so* worth it.

Simple… Powerful… Profound.

5.

Be Still and Know

We're all hurting in so many ways. Life knocks us around a lot and inevitably we all end up with our share of scars and bruises: physical, mental, and emotional.

Just not being scared for a while can mean so much. But with so much coming at you, how do you manage to drop your defenses? How do you remember life is supposed to be a grand adventure, at least most of the time?

You've got to relax. You've got to chill. Sometimes nothing is the very best thing you can do. Be still? Here in the West, we revere industry above all else. In America, industry rules the day. How many times have you heard (or said), "I can't, I have to work." The world of *that* kind of work is a noisy, busy one. It has been said that there is nothing so much like the voice of God as silence. Yet we in the modern world know little of silence or stillness.

The reality is that the roar and rattle of life in the cities and towns where most of us live captures our attention so completely that we simply forget the empty stillness in which it all happens. The Buddhists call it "The Pure Land." The Chinese masters call it Wu Chi. I call it the Qigong state. It is the perfection of what is, before it starts moving, before it starts breathing, it is the subtle sensibility that all that noise assaults.

6.

It's All in How You See It

Of all the symbols that have come my way, none have represented our situation more clearly than this:

    The old Taoists simply called it the way. The way to what, you ask? The way it is, they'd say. How can I know that's true you ask? Test it. Embody it, they'd say. Practice balancing the Yin and Yang of life. Breath goes in, breath goes out. Tense - relax. Expand – contract. Nowhere to go. Nothing to do. It arises. It subsides. It is what it is. Forever – Life Eternal. Be still and know.

    Over the years, so many times when I'd be lost in one of life's tangles, the question would arise, "What *is* this?" In that moment the answer would flash into my Mind:

    See it from here

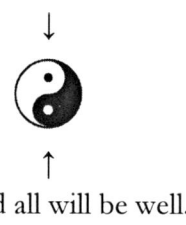

And all will be well.

7.

What Dreams May Come

Life is mysterious, magical, miraculous, and unfathomable.

As Shakespeare so eloquently put it, "There are more things in heaven and earth dear Horatio, than are dreamt of in your philosophy." Philosophy and history for that matter are merely some individual's interpretation of events masquerading as knowledge, speculations presented as facts.

But then if we are purely objective about our place in the cosmos, human nature being what it is, we would live our lives in abject terror as we hurtle through the void at the mind numbing speed of 660,000 mph aboard a highly unstable little sphere where a thousand subtle forces are held in a momentary fragile balance. Should they shift, just a little – Poof! – We're gone. But man oh man - What a ride! Some hold on tight. Some like it best with their hands in the air.

It has been said in many traditions that life is like a dream, but there are different kinds of dreams. There are haunting dreams playing out deeply unconscious scenarios in endlessly creative ways. There are fantastic dreams in which the rules and laws of the past no longer apply. There are nightmares where the world rushes headlong toward disaster, and the child-like dreams of wishes magically coming true.

They exist, as us, through us, in combinations beyond imagining. Presently, about six billion plus, and yet all of them together are only a drop in the great cosmic bucket.

It feels like chaos. And yet, there is a subtle intelligence underlying it all. It isn't a bad thing. It isn't a good thing. It's just the way it is, and there's just one thing to do – wake up and realize you have been dreaming. You have a hand in creating it all. Take some responsibility. Become skillful in playing your part. It's grand theatre, a cosmic opera of 6 billion voices. And yet, the show can't go on without you.

You are not Life's victim. You are its process and its purpose all at once.

8.

What You See Is What You Get

What is enlightenment? That question has haunted me for decades. At first it brought with it only more questions. Is it real? Do I really want it? What can I do to get there? Where is there?

As a young man I thought I could get there (quite a few times) with psychedelic substances. However, like Timothy Leary and Richard Alpert of *Be Here Now* fame, I found I could only wander the strangely beautiful world of hallucinations and visions and it was still up to me to judge them real or not, reliant completely upon my inherent ability to discern which was which. The experience served the purpose of showing me that I was indeed the infinitely creative source of my experience of the world, but little else. Drugs don't get you anywhere, at least not where enlightenment is concerned. Enlightenment does not consist of *what* you see, but *how* you see. That single revelation, of being the source of the world, the conscious observer, has been the focal point of a decades long quest. What is the source of the world? Where does all of this come from?

The play of consciousness masquerading as opposites each magically defining the other is the process. The mind identifying one as real, the other as not, is where things start to go terribly wrong. Is clear seeing really possible? What do you think?

9.

Enlightenment - Not As Rare As You Think

What was it that happened to Lord Krishna, Gautama, Jesus, Moses, and Muhammad? How was it that these men were consumed in Holy fire and emerged as something more than men? Were they precursors of what we all will one day be? Did they simply see and affirm what is possible for us all?

They weren't the only ones, I eventually discovered, only the most lauded. There have been hundreds, thousands probably, who awoke to a new reality, and then just lived out their lives in some obscure corner of the world. Without the printing press and widespread literacy, mass communication and ease of travel in the modern world, what would we know of the Zen patriarchs or Lao Tsu, author of the most translated work after the bible, the *Tao Te Ching*. Who would have ever heard of Ramana Maharshi living out his life in a little hut at the foot of Arunachala Hill; or Nisargadatta Maharaj giving talks in the cramped little loft over his Cigarette shop in Bombay? How many God intoxicated souls have walked the earth in each and every generation throughout all of human history?

What is this innate impulse unique to human beings to be something more? What is this peace beyond understanding, this quest for unclouded knowing, we are endlessly compelled to pursue, however mistaken and misguided our efforts become?

These are the questions that have haunted me as long as I can remember. They will not let me go.

Somehow, sooner or later we each sense this something that wants desperately to become. Andrew Cohen, the founder of *What Is Enlightenment* magazine calls it the evolutionary impulse. Good name.

Now the mind thinks it knows, "The evolutionary impulse – of course!"

"Oh God," I sigh to that mysterious something out there somewhere.

"What?" answers a still small voice within, and I'm stunned into silence.

It is from that silence that *everything* emerges. It is the silence between the notes that allows the rhythms and pulse of the music to be heard. It is the empty space between the words that allows us to discern them, the empty sheet of paper that permits them to appear. It is the vast emptiness that is the foundation through which the entire universe flies; and so it is with each of us. We are the space and emptiness into which all perceptions, thoughts, feelings and subtle sensibilities are born; all of them silent and invisible, yet very, very real. What an incredible miracle emptiness is.

10.

The Zombies Want YOU!

Whenever trouble or problems arise we tend to focus our attention in that direction. An energetic tension arises. That tension resonates with other tensions from the past in an effort to create a 'knowing' of what's happening, creating a feeling of even more anxiety and tension in the body. That anxiety and tension create a stronger focus on problems and trouble, which in turn create more anxious thoughts and man, now you *are* in trouble! You can't see anything else! And what you're seeing is the dead past coming back to life.

What you need to do is quit feeling like you're starring in *The Night of the Living Dead*. Use your natural agility to put a little distance between you and the zombies. They're unconscious, you are not. They are *not* good company. Dinner invitations are no longer appropriate.

To be comfortable we require a certain amount of physical space. We require a certain amount of emotional and mental space as well. When things start getting a little too crowded, it's time to move. Whenever you feel like you're stuck and there's no way out. Don't buy it. It's an illusion, a trick of the mind. Relax, breathe & move. The solution is simple. Seeing it is not. Quit feeding the fire. Step back from the heat. Go for a walk. Let the embers cool.

Sometimes in the middle of a Qigong set, as that feeling of well-being begins to replace whatever else was there. I find myself marveling just for a moment, "Who *were* these guys? How did they come up with this stuff?" What a wonderfully, gloriously simple thing. Relax, breathe, move - watch and feel. The result is always the same - more life - real life. Not problems. Not troubles – Life.

11.

It's Different Every Time

I have been enlightened many times. There have been retreats that have been so powerful that going back to old routines seemed like that scene from *The African Queen* when 'Bogie' bravely climbs overboard once again, into the swamp from which he had just emerged moments before, discovering himself covered with leeches, and he *hates* leeches. O.K, perhaps I'm exaggerating just a tad, but it was hard.

I've seen sunsets so beautiful that they have made me weep for joy. I have been blessed to be in the presence of teachers whose connection to Being was so strong that I found myself swept effortlessly into the moment, leaving who and what I thought I was far behind. For a while…

The best of them often showing seekers the way to a grander view just by asking the right question at the right time; shedding a bit of light upon whatever seemingly insurmountable obstacle happened to be barring their way; revealing how insubstantial it really was. And having set their feet firmly upon the path once more, graciously stepped aside.

When you're open, that's when miracles happen, or more correctly, that's when you see what's happening for the miracle it is. It happens so easily when the mind is quiet enough. Simply letting things be instead of manically trying to turn everything into something that happened before. Just so it can feel like it knows. Sucking the life out of every new moment, every new experience, turning the wondrous shining present instantly into a dusty relic of a long dead past. "Oh, I know this, it's just like that"… murdering the present, turning miracles to mud. (viewing life through filters of self-interest, Steven would say.)

There are two ways out. One, you have to be lucky enough to be in the presence of a teacher who will remind you again and again, "Did you see what just happened?" bringing it immediately to your attention. (People don't follow these guys around for nothing, you know.) Two, you find a way to disconnect from being such a pushover for that voice in your head. Instead of being so smug about it, just so you can think that you know, be present enough to ask the question yourself, "Is that true?" (Byron Katie has written a wonderful book on this that might help establish the habit called, *Loving What Is*.)

In either case one must be committed to seeing more clearly. To see anything you have to be watching. Learn to watch. Don't analyze, compare, judge, think; just watch. It's a skill that must be developed. It's a skill you develop with Qigong.

12.

Be the Big Hermit

Many years ago I came across the statement, "You are the center of the universe."

"Oh great," I thought. (As you may have guessed, this was during my cynical phase.) "Just what the world needs, more hubris." In those days everywhere I looked, especially in my own life, being the center of the universe was not a revelation. Thinking that I was, was the fundamental problem. Forgive me, but I've changed my mind.

This process of awakening that we inevitably experience, even if we're kicking and screaming all the way, is a messy affair and there's nothing we can do about that.

Justin Stone, the originator of T'ai Chi Chih used to ask, "Are you the big hermit or the little hermit? The little hermit lives a simple life, meditating in the quiet of the hermitage. The big hermit meditates and lives a simple life in the middle of the hustle and bustle of the marketplace. Who of the two will more easily lose his peace?"

Take your average monk, bring him into mainstream society, give him a 50 hour work week in some mindless corporation with an hour commute each way, a wife, a couple of kids, and a 30 year mortgage on a house built decades ago in the suburbs and he'd be on his way to a nervous breakdown before you could say Om Mané Padme Hum.

However, I have to admit, the experiences of Vietnam, blowing out my knee, going bankrupt, getting divorced, and drinking way too much for my own good for a while, in addition to raising five sons, has been a very enlightening indeed. Though it sure didn't feel like it while I was going through it. While I can sympathize if you're inclined to put a "Life Sucks" bumper sticker on your car, it doesn't.

The fact of the matter is, you *are* the center of the universe. *You* are the process of awakening. Everything "bad" that happens to you is just the alarm going off – "Time to Wake Up!" You are far more than you think you are. You are not your job, your relationships, your (ahem!) slightly overweight body. You are an instrument of the awakening universe. It is seeing itself through your eyes, feeling itself through your heart. Without you there would be nothing but "Darkness upon the deep."

13.

A Deep Reverence for Life

You are endlessly creative. Think of what you thought life was about ten years ago, and now? Look at how your relationships have changed, the subtle ways your body has changed, for better or worse. Change is. One fundamental criteria that I'd highly recommend you pay attention to is this - is it in accord with a deep reverence for life? I think it was Neale Donald Walsh in his *Conversations with God* series that hit me over the head with that one. "Do you have a deep reverence for life?"

"Of course," I inwardly answered.

He went on to say, "If you smoke cigarettes, you do not have a deep reverence for life." I squirmed. "If you drink alcohol on a regular basis, you do not have a deep reverence for life".

"Hey buddy, what's your problem?" I thought.

"If you use drugs to get high, you do not have a deep reverence for life."

"OK, I've had just about enough of this. Now I'm pissed. Why didn't anyone mention this little dialog was sponsored by the vice squad?" I still remember how upset I was. That was a long time ago.

After practicing these silly little movements over and over again, I don't smoke. I don't drink. I don't do drugs. I honor and revere this life for the miracle it is. Go figure.

14.

The Path to Real Power.

Let Go. Relax, Breathe, Feel. My wife Cori, teaches women to birth their babies that way. She has developed a system that facilitates painless childbirth. She teaches that labor pains aren't pains at all, but intense squeezing. They're awesomely powerful contractions, it's true, but they aren't pains. Pain is the body's natural expression to alert us that something is wrong. So much of what we perceive as pain and suffering is what we experience when we're afraid of what's happening. It lies at the heart of the feeling that something is wrong. What's wrong in both cases is not allowing "what is" to be. When resistance becomes monumental, the pain can seem unbearable. Let go. Don't resist. Your challenge is to remember to relax and breathe in the middle of all that is assailing you. Feel it deeply. Don't waste a single moment wishing it were not so. It's only life having its way with you. It's birthing something. Let it come. It's part of what you're here to do.

15.

It's Not Supposed to Make You Crazy

Few people have ever even heard of Qigong. (I'm working on it!) The word is usually met with a blank stare. The spelling certainly doesn't help matters, so I'm going to offer it up in all its known forms. Qigong is Chi Kung. It's also Chi gung, which is how it's pronounced no matter how you choose to spell it.

Chi (Qi), pronounced Chee is the life force, the vital force that mysteriously animates all living things. Gong, pronounced gung, is practice or cultivation. More specifically, it is a persistent cultivation of a skill with the ultimate goal of mastering it. Chi gung is becoming so intimate with that intelligent organizing principle that you begin to experience yourself in the light of something more wise and vast than you can possibly imagine, and learning to open and allow its free expression through you. Why? - to satisfy your innate impulse to be free - truly free.

On one level, life is a crazy, confusing, hodge-podge of experiences, moods, emotions and physical challenges that change places willy-nilly upon the back drop of an ever-changing scene.

A cultivated attitude of free-flowing acceptance really helps to keep things in proper perspective. When we spend a little time and energy becoming more intimate with the simple tools of body, breath, and movement (and paradoxically, stillness) we gain a much more reliable point of view.

You are not a leaf in the wind. You are a part of the tree of life, rooted in the earth, open to the rule of heaven, faithfully performing your role in the flow of life for a season. It's not supposed to make you crazy. There is great joy inherent in it.

As Tony Parsons says, "Life is its own purpose. It doesn't need a reason to be." It is. You are. It's the one thing you know without question. Whether you realize it or not, you are the universe awakening to the experience of itself. Your mind is designed in accord with its Mind. As I've stated time and again, it's looking out through your eyes. It feels with your heart. Without the light of your consciousness, there would be no 'knowing' of any of it. Can you imagine what a terribly lonely and senseless thing such a creation would be?

An ancient Hindu sutra says:

> *Not that which I think,*
> *but that whereby I can think.*
> *This alone I call Brahman the eternal,*
> *and not what people here adore.*
> *Not that which I hear,*
> *but that whereby I can hear.*
> *This alone I call Brahman the eternal,*
> *and not what people here adore.*
> *Not that which I see,*
> *but that whereby I can see.*
> *This alone I call Brahman the eternal,*
> *and not what people here adore.*

16.

Cease to Cherish Opinions

I have a friend, or more accurately a co-worker for whom I have a certain fondness. He lives in a world of black and white. He loves to say things like, "If you don't' stand for something, you'll fall for anything." He has a flag pole flying Old Glory in the front yard of his modest house. He thinks my Qigong practice is un-American.

Like the suit and tied pairs that wander my neighborhood on Sundays spreading the "Good News" or handing out copies of the *Watch Tower* to any and all, he's grown comfortable in embracing a certain limited view of life.

It's black and white alright, yin and yang gloriously expressing as mind. The trick is to be discerning enough to see the way each defines the other without making a "something" out of it. It is easier said than done. The leaps from black and white, to dark and light, to evil and good, are far too readily made. Somehow we've got to avoid being sucked into picking a side, convinced that we are truly making a choice.

"There is only Yang!!"

"Yin is irrelevant!"

This is the kind of trap the mind is endlessly setting. How do we get caught time and again in something so obviously absurd? Don't fall for it. Life is a thousand shades of grey. Reducing the complexity of the world to black or white results in one thing only, someone's going to get hurt. Whenever you find yourself arguing a certain point of view, or taking a stand, you're caught. Stop. Freedom is just one short step away. Shut up. Then ask yourself, "What am I defending? – And why?"

17.

We Are One

It is a fine line that we walk in our journey toward greater freedom. There is the distinct possibility inherent in whatever unconventional things we may explore, that we will subtly revel in just being different. Qigong practice is the most natural thing in the world. It's not going to make you 'special'. It's going to reveal to you what you *truly* are. It's going to wake you up.

We live in a time when everything of value from any culture on earth is available to us through books, TV and the internet. Here in the good ol' USA we are particularly fortunate that people come from all over the world and bring their culture's treasures with them to their new home. America has its own tradition of allowing them (and us) to express ourselves freely, providing fertile ground for hybrids of the old and new to emerge. This is the true spirit of American Qigong. It is our birthright. It's what naturally occurs as we open and allow this life force to express itself more freely in the world.

Human nature is transcendent. We live upon and are born of the earth, but the realm of the heart is the stuff of heaven. Our bodies say we are separate. Our hearts know we are One. We have but one source, and one experience, the human experience. We all see, touch, taste, smell and hear. You would never think to say, "I can taste and you cannot." We all know the simple joy of sharing a sweet treat with another. Why then would we ever think for a moment that another cannot know our pain, sadness, joy, or fear? Why would we ever hurt another knowing how hurt feels? Furthermore, how could anyone being hurt ever say, "Forgive them for they know not what they do?" Only through a deep knowing that it's not personal. Thinking that it is, is by and large, what causes most of the pain.

18.

Breathe!

When my son Caleb was 14, He came up with this joke:

"Sometimes I think that confusion is the source of all happiness…

Confused? Good!"

Here is a simple way to dispel confusion and worry; a simple way to leave tiresome repetitious thoughts behind, and open to new possibilities. The next time you're caught in a 'sit & spin' put one palm lightly on your heart, the other just above your navel. Relax your shoulders. Feel them drop as you exhale. Feel your belly expand on the inhale, softly collapsing on the exhale. Imagine that the lungs are in the belly instead of the chest, like there is a balloon in your belly inflating – deflating – inflating again. Relax the body a little more with every exhale. The same way you'd let a subtle sigh soften you as you sit on the edge of your bed after a trying day. Inhale 2 – 3 – 4, exhale 2 – 3 – 4, again 2 – 3 – 4, exhale 2 - 3 - 4, stay with it awhile. Let the breath flow easily in and out, through the nose; smooth, fine, deep and even. Watch it… feel it… think to yourself, "with each exhalation comes deeper and deeper relaxation." Feel it happening. Let go of thought for a while. Let go of tension. Just breathe. Whenever you feel tension in the body, let this be your response.

Clarity is coming. Be patient… Relax… Let it come…

19.

Negative Energy

From where does our happiness come? It comes from within. What causes it to arise? Often it is the relief of tension. From where does negativity arise? From resistance to what is. Let it be. Don't let unconscious inclinations pick and choose. Don't allow mind to separate and negate. There's room in the world for all of it. When resistance to any experience arises, don't feed it with negative thought. Don't start judging it. Just breathe deeply; relaxing with each exhalation, and watch it. See it for what it is, relax to the best of your ability and let it be. If you don't feed it, it will go away. Let it go. Resistance is encouraging life energy to tighten into a knot. It is a 'flow' of energy congealing into a 'thing' seeking a subtle aliveness through being fed by you.

It's completely natural of course. It's not a good thing; it's not a bad thing. It is simply the way of subtle energy. Harmonize with it. See how it moves inside of you – wanting to become a part of you, searching for a place to hold on to.

Be gentle; be compassionate, but firm. Just say no. Relax, breathe, and as the tension unravels and flows, you will feel a subtle satisfaction in your accomplishment. Great joy results from such subtle accomplishments when repeated often enough. This is often referred to as 'energy work'. Increasing skill is born of practice. Such a skill is more valuable than you realize. It is 'work' of the very best kind.

20.

Rest

Sometimes you're just tired… spent. There is no energy available to fuel the day's plans. At such times, it is important to recognize the situation for what it is and not force upon it whatever weak responses we can muster to push bravely on. This too, is letting go.

We too often think that progress is as much about fits and starts, passion filled marathons withering to exhaustion; running jumps that miss their mark and rubber-legged stumbles that we arise from, shivering, disheveled and soaked to the skin; as it is about ultimately punching into the air, victorious in our accomplishment. Know when it is time to rest. Don't give up – but in choosing to press relentlessly on there is great potential for ruin. It is important to know when to be still. Be wise. You can't push the river. Go with the flow, and use such opportunities to rebuild your strength and vitality and *then* continue on.

There will be times when nothing can be done. There is great power in recognizing such moments and responding accordingly. Be skilled in your pursuits. Know that your own exhaustion is the only thing that will defeat you. Know that there will be times when *nothing* is the very best thing to do. Know when it's time to rest.

All movement rests upon the potential energies that inexorably build in stillness. Rest assured that your intent alone is sufficient to marshal those forces that will eventually burst forth, unstoppable, in their own time. In this way your purposes will find the most effortless way into becoming. Harmonize with the process. Patience always succeeds. This is what is truly meant by "timing is everything".

21.

Never-Ending Creation

It is not uncommon for a dedicated Qigong practitioner to feel from time to time like a strange visitor from another planet with powers far beyond those of mortal men. There is a touch of the miraculous in this daily visiting of realms of subtle (and sometimes not so subtle) energies; uncovering layer upon layer of emotionally charged experiences whose echoes somehow constitute this edifice of "me" and "how I am". What amazing artifice! What incredible creativity! What a magnificent delusion. Though it happens just this way, but once, there are six billion variations simultaneously on display upon this tiny orb of outrageous possibilities. Is it even possible that there is some greater purpose playing itself out? Or is it that "it is" is the be all and end all at once? Who can say?

> The Mystery
> The mind cannot grasp it,
> the body holds it dear
> This living, moving, consciousness
> untouched by death, or doubt,
> or fear
>
> Within life's eternal moment
> we see and hear, touch, taste and feel
> through a perfect, shining, nothingness,
> the source and ground of all that's real.
>
> Love's pulse creating endlessly
> not just this wondrous
> world of ours, but
> four hundred billion galaxies,
> of a hundred billion stars.

22.

What Is Enlightenment?

Enlightenment is moving beyond Yin & Yang while allowing them to be.

It is being present for joy's arising from the silent stillness in which it resides.

Enlightenment is the end of suffering, it is the before and after of thought, it is freedom from accumulated knowledge and the freshness of knowing.

It is the seeing of what was always there for the very first time.

Enlightenment is being as miserable as ever and embracing it with loving compassion.

It is watching old structures crumble (as they must) and building nothing in their place.

Enlightenment is a willing abandonment of the known, allowing the possibility of choiceless awareness.

It is the end of self-reliance and the birth of Self-reliance.

Enlightenment is opening to the ever-expanding creation expressing as you and willingly becoming the instrument through which the ever-expanding creation can live in ways it could not without you.

It is the recognition of what you, and others, and the world truly are, and loving all of it.

Enlightenment is holding the realization firmly in your heart and mind that beyond all appearances –

"There is spirit alone in the universe. There is no second thing in existence."

~ Lord Krishna

23.

Who Was Jesus Really?

In the modern world one is bombarded constantly from all sides with stimuli that are at war with stillness, opposed to peace.

Our attention is the precious treasure that is the envy of the ten thousand things that will vie for it every moment of our lives. To what and whom will we give it? Will it simply be taken by forces grown powerful within and without? These things are determined by you and you alone.

First, we must recognize that our attention is the foundation of all our experience. This lies at the heart of all realization. Being aware that you are aware is the first step in waking from the dream. Awareness IS. It doesn't come from your brain or your senses, it is that from which your brain and your senses arise. It is the "Secret of Life" in plain sight, masquerading as nothing at all.

It is my suspicion that when Jesus the Christ said, "I am the Way and the Truth and the Life. None can come to the father (the creative intelligence) but through me," he was speaking *as pure awareness*. What other people saw and heard was a "person" speaking, and saw him as a blasphemer, or even worse – the one and only son of God. Fortunately, there were those with hearts open enough to 'feel' what he truly was. If they could just refrain from judging things from appearances (conceptual thought) and just love (be at one with) him and their fellow men, by simply forgiving themselves and others for getting so caught in mind (the law) they could eventually become free of its influence. This is the teaching.

Awareness IS. Awareness is the Way things become things. That's the Truth. It's what "life" is: The eternal process of awareness becoming aware of itself. The fulfillment of this possibility depends on us, you and I.

However, it's so subtle, so elusive, that all it takes is being hungry or angry (or oh so logical) and - Poof! It's gone.

So we must practice remaining "awareness" above all else. It lies at the heart of Yogananda's expansive "Center everywhere, circumference nowhere," perspective. We have to consciously practice being less easily distracted, less easily dissipated into identifying with the ten thousand things arising endlessly within and without. Fortunately, this isn't as hard as it sounds. It just requires persistence. It's a matter of gaining the skills required to maintain the proper point of view. The sole requirement is being willing to continually pay attention to what you're paying attention to in order to gain, and then support, a less selfish, more universal perspective. We must be dedicated to nurturing our ability to "see" more clearly with unwavering tenacity. It is through this persistent effort that we prepare ourselves to receive grace – assured of its coming. As Joan Tollifson states in her book *Awake in the Heartland*, "Grace is in the seeing, not the situation." What a fine affirmation of our potential for transformation. Transcend the perceived limits of the situation. Open and accord with Grace. And your expanded vision will set you free.

To spend a portion of every day unconscious is our lot by nature. It happens every night whether we want it to or not, but waking up is also our lot. This too happens all by itself. Ultimately though, how awake or unconscious we choose to be becomes a matter of personal choice. The degree for each determined by whether we are addicted to the drama of our soap opera lives, or truly desire to experience greater joy, peace and love. All three are attributes of greater awareness. The more aware you are, the more they appear in your life. It's that simple.

24.

The Big Picture

There are at least five levels of development occurring simultaneously whenever one practices Qigong. These are: the physical, mental, emotional, spiritual and behavioral levels of life. In putting the last first we acquire our most valuable skill - discipline. Most people upon seeing or hearing the word, equate it with punishment. Discipline is not punishment. Discipline is about integrity. It is through discipline that you learn to do what you mean to do, say what you mean to say, and become what you mean to be. It is living honestly, with integrity. It is living in a balanced way.

We've all been through hell in one way or another, probably more than once. And we bear the mental and emotional scars to prove it. Our approach to life, what it is, what it means, our place in it, is colored by those emotionally charged experiences that have been relegated to our unconscious mind. That's where our conditioned responses (habitual unconscious reactions) come from. The subconscious is running the show whenever you don't have to think for a moment (how convenient!) about what to do, you just do it. They are essentially energy pathways, or grooves, in our psyche that we find ourselves operating from again and again. The ancient Vedic texts call them vrittis – habit energies.

Of all of the forces regulating our lives, one of the most powerful is habit. The fact that you have tried to change the way you feel; the way you think; the way you eat; how much you weigh; your relationship with your father – and failed – is because this is so. It's not because you're weak, it's because you answer to a far more formidable master. The force of habit has been ingrained in us for a million years (and then some!). So the first order of business it to get this powerful force on the side of our desire for change. Qigong is not a weekend seminar or workshop. It is a daily practice. It is a discipline.

Luckily, it has a number of things going for it that make it a little more user-friendly than most.
1. It's pretty easy.
2. It doesn't hurt.
3. It always feels good.
4. It doesn't take a lot of time.
5. It doesn't cost a lot of money.

Most importantly, it accomplishes so much for the little time and energy it requires, you might feel a little silly when you are inclined to 'blow it off'. My advice? - Don't.

The easiest way to get it going is to pick a half hour somewhere in the day (morning or evening being best) and assign that time to "Being the best I can be". If that's what you want. And seeing as how you've stayed with me this far, I'd say chances are pretty good that *is* what you want. Otherwise, you'd probably be having a beer. (Come to think of it, maybe you *are* having a beer! I used to do that, read spiritual stuff while having a drink – doesn't work.) Maybe you're having a bowl of ice cream, or another piece (or two) of chocolate cake. There's nothing *wrong* with any of it. All of those things will make you feel good – for a while. But who knows, it just might become a habit!

Know this – it won't make you feel as good as a little qigong practice. Believe me, I'm speaking from experience. All of the above have their consequences. Choose wisely. The trick is to get the force of habit working for you not against you.

Achieving this very first goal is, in and of itself, wonderfully empowering. Be someone who does what they say they're going to do. Set your intent in stone. Make a vow. It sets you apart from the person who says "I've tried, but I just can't". Don't you feel your heart sink a little whenever you hear someone say those words? I do. Encountering resignation is always such a sad state of affairs.

Regarding discipline, that little green fictional character, Master Yoda in *Star Wars* said it short and to the point, "Do or do not, there is no try". Regular practice of anything is strengthening your power of intent. It is deeply satisfying to 'walk your talk'. All too easily life can become a murky muddle of "should've... would've... could've." The simple act of walking your talk creates a different world within, and so a very different world without. Ultimately, the fact that you regularly practice any sacred technology changes not just you, it changes the world. It is an act of 'Enlightened Self-Interest' to become a more perfect instrument through which life affirming influences find their way into the physical world. You have the capacity to introduce subtle creative impulses into the mix that would not be possible without you. And all the while, those influences operating within will bring you the gifts of greater health and energy, mental and emotional well-being, and more sustained episodes of joy and peace.

We are catalysts of change. The world needs you to change in ways it cannot without you. We are its own children grown to parenthood. We are the mediators between the forces of heaven and earth.

So far our collective track record isn't that great. Ego and mind centered, we remain totally self-absorbed. Egoic concerns and blatant self-interest make us woefully inadequate stewards of creation. They are products of it, to be sure. But while expedient, that they've allowed us to survive as a species until now, they have outlived their usefulness as the primary movers in the human condition. We're all just a little crazy. Multiply that by six billion and that's *a lot* of crazy. It's time to put away childish things and move on to a more mature approach to life. It's not all about what *we* want. It's about discovering what we are. Blatant, willful self-interest must be set aside.

The egoic mind of man simply doesn't have the capacity to even begin to comprehend the far vaster intelligence expressing as the integrated complex structures supporting life on planet earth. Man's mind is endlessly separating and analyzing parts of the whole. Ego is obsessed with expressing individuality. But the real answers to all of our seeking lie in the other direction. Whenever we act on a part of something seeing it as the whole, we naively set forces in motion that have consequences (for good or ill) upon all that we fail to see. Ego is always about personal gratification. Truly appropriate actions require a much wider scope. Adroitly merging with ever-expanding awareness isn't just a good idea – It's the Law!

"*...And it harm none, do what thou wilt*"

– An old Wiccan saying

25.

War and Peace

I am a veteran of the war in Vietnam. I have been known to reply to the inquiry, "Were you in Vietnam?" with the response "Wasn't everybody?" Just to gently remind myself that, of course, everybody wasn't. A few million of us were, out of a nation of 300 million. That's not a lot. In war nasty things happen. People are reduced to chunks; innocents (*lots* of innocents) get hurt and killed, and the majority of the people involved are not on their best behavior. War is insane. You have to cope.

In a war you are forced to adapt certain behaviors just to get through it. If you've never seen the movie *Platoon*, I highly recommend it to anyone curious about what those behaviors might be. It's tough to maintain your humanity in a war. "Kill'em all and let God sort'em out," seems somehow reasonably justifiable. Perhaps that's why there are enough nukes in the world to destroy us all a hundred times over. Yet, somehow that too seems reasonably justifiable.

In our daily lives we often have smaller wars going on inside. Outrageous solutions to our problems arise that have a certain appeal and yet, they're just as insane as the Wars going on outside. In any war even the winner loses. How in the world does such craziness manage to take hold of us? It only seems to make sense when you're waaay out of balance.

Is punching someone in the face really a valid response to an insult? Is killing someone because you want their land, or their stuff, or because they don't see things the same way you do, really a valid option? Would the world be a better place without killers? Of course it would - Let's kill'em all! Do you see how strangely reasonable that sounds? It is *not* reasonable! It is madness! It's a visceral response. Something deeply unconscious is making you do it. It feels as if you have no choice - and you're right. You only have a choice when you are conscious of what you're doing. You have to be awake to *see* what you're doing. Most people are unconscious most of the time. There ought to be a bumper sticker: "Unconsciousness Kills!" Though I'm afraid most people wouldn't get it. Wake up! Notice how it's often your own woundedness that makes you want to say and do hurtful things. If you see it in yourself, you will have a greater capacity to forgive it in others. This is the only way to move toward peace in the world.

If someone does you harm, forgive them, see them as innocent and you'll automatically stop killing them in your mind. Know that they're sleepwalking. They look like they're awake, but it's an illusion. They really don't know what they're doing. It's coming from a place inside of them that hasn't seen the light of their awareness in years. They really don't have a choice - yet. In loving them (seeing them as yourself) at least *you* wake up to the realization that what you're feeling and thinking is more about what's happening in you than in them, and *that* you can do something about.

The first order of business is always: Wake up! Shine the light of awareness into your own dark corners. Second, do whatever it takes to *stay* awake. Be consistent. Then, as you meet with some success, build on it. Whenever the opportunity presents itself, share those insights with others. We can help each other awaken. In some teachings it is said that in truth there *are* no others; that *your* experience and *my* experience are not personal; that there is in fact, only the human experience unfolding from two different points of view.

I like that. I like that very much.

26.

Home Sweet Home

A short time after my father died I was reflecting on his life and our relationship. In trying to sort it all out all hell broke loose. I saw that countless emotional and mental mechanisms that had found a permanent home in my internal landscape had come into being just to deal with him. My dad was, to say the least, an extremely unbalanced person. I suspect he may have been what is now called Bipolar. For many years I simply called it "card – carrying crazy."

(True story: In his later years, following an episode of temporary dementia brought on by a drug interaction, he was given a little card by his Dr. that said if he was acting crazy to call the emergency number on the card. - I knew it!)

He was without exception the most foul-mouthed man I ever knew. My brother and I would sometimes give ourselves the giggles in recounting how many cuss words he could fit into a sentence. During one of his diatribes, we were so overcome with suppressed laughter at breakfast one morning that my brother Jim, no longer able to contain himself, shot a substantial blast of Rice Krispies out of his nose, (peppering the area so completely that we were picking dried on Krispies off of everything for days) at which point I too completely lost control and we both couldn't stop laughing and my father only made it worse raising the bar on swearing without taking a breath to stratospheric levels while pummeling us both. …Breakfast at the Nielsen house.

My father almost always preferred his colorful descriptions of us in lieu of our actual names. More than once our horrified neighbors could take no more and would ask him to stop, whereupon he would proceed to tell them equally colorfully not only how little he cared, but where they could take their opinions, and what they could do with them once they got there.

He lied all the time. At the time, I had no idea why. Which was very confusing because it was also one of his favorite reasons for stripping off his belt in a lightning-quick fit of rage. "You God-damned little LIAR!!" he'd bellow, and just start swinging. He was just mean, junkyard dog mean. Sometimes just seeing you pissed him off. Stoned cold sober, sitting at the kitchen table, if he caught you looking at him, like some surly drunk in a bar, he'd sneer in a too loud voice, "What're *you* lookin' at?"

He somehow had his signals crossed. He wasn't mean to people out in the world. He was only that way with his wife and kids, the only people who cared about him at all. Just like the Grinch, he so reveled in being sinister that I'd sometimes catch him exhibiting a sickeningly smug, self-satisfied grin at his own creativity in coming up with some new means of mentally torturing us all. He would often reiterate how much he disliked having to mete out physical punishment upon whatever family member had trespassed against him. I always suspected that underlying it all there was but one reason - he was continuously outraged at how one of us kids was always stealing away the love that should have been his. As a result, whenever my mother wasn't around, there was hell to pay. His incessant irritation, and cruelty to us kids inevitably served to increasingly distance her from him – and 'round and 'round we all went - Home Sweet Home.

As with most walking wounded, he wasn't all bad. Curiously, he had a reputation for being an easy touch for those with a good sob story. Those fortunate recipients of his favor ever after looked upon him as a 'Good Joe.' Though I suspect there was a subtle feeling of being better than all of them at the root of his generosity. He had a sharp mind, but not much humor. He liked arguing, and was very good at it. He could beat you up with words. I often think he would have made an exceptionally fine lawyer. Yet, if any one of us kids or my mother was holding our own during one of his verbal assaults, he was not at all shy about getting physical to once again gain the upper hand.

I never once saw him do that in the world of men. If he got carried away and pursued his verbal attack too aggressively invoking the ire of his target, he would very quickly become apologetic, even flattering, to avoid getting clobbered.

I must admit, for a while, the perverse art of verbal assault was one of the things in which I surpassed my teacher, much to his chagrin. As I grew in size and physical strength and getting physical was no longer an option, my father began to deeply resent having played all his best cards so early and finding himself out of the game, (Though it brought him joy to watch me do it to others.) There was a certain twisted pride in it, I think. In that sense the apple hadn't fallen far from the tree.

I was the oldest. When I finally confronted him about our strained relationship, He confessed to never liking me because I always acted like I thought I was better than him. Imagine a grown man feeling that way about a child. In turn, I disliked him because I knew he was never better than me, just bigger. I just wanted him to love me. To be honest I don't know if he ever really knew what love was, or how to express it. Toward the end of his life, after my mother died, whenever I hugged him he'd stiffen up like a board. He didn't know what to do.

On the upside, in dealing with my father, I learned to trust my feelings, my perceptions, myself. I rarely sought counsel, (for better or worse). That was his gift to me that I couldn't fully appreciate at the time. In many ways, simply by being who he was he instilled in me what not to be. It's why I don't ever purposely hurt anyone; if I do, I will not let pride stand in the way of asking forgiveness. Eventually, in healing my hard heartedness towards him for all he was not, I found the ability to more readily forgive myself and others. I also recognize crazy. I can sense hidden pain, even in strangers. In many ways he was a fine teacher indeed.

Then, one day he died. He was gone and yet I still had all this stuff that I came up with to deal with life with father. I lied about things to make myself feel better. Very angry people seemed normal to me. I eventually married one and it felt comfortably familiar until it finally dawned on me (shortly after I started practicing Qigong) what was really going on. That's another one of those times when all hell broke loose.

Throughout my teens and early twenties I stubbornly resisted just about everything I was told to do by anyone. I had a real problem with authority. (You can imagine how well that went over when I got drafted.) My father was gone, I was still here, and I feared from time to time, that I'd end up as crazy as he was.

Then there was Mom. Mom was a waitress most of my life. Then she graduated to a cook. She discovered that cooks have more power. She reveled in appreciation. Tell her thanks, give her a hug and a kiss and you could pretty much have anything you wanted. All of her kids loved that about her. So did the guys at the bar. Yes, Mom was also a bit of a barfly. She was basically a good person and a lousy judge of character.

Mom died first. She passed away of renal failure after being unconscious in the ICU for days. I cried when I heard she was gone. Her life seemed so sad to me. She told me a story more than once, of what I believe defined her to a great degree.

Her mother left her and her older brother to live with her sister in Gary, Indiana while she worked all week in Chicago as a hospital dietician. I have no idea of what her father did, or even the kind of man her father was. Strangely, the subject was verboten. I have no recollection of anyone in her family ever even mentioning him. Her mother took an apartment in the city. At first, she would come to visit on Sundays a couple of times a month to see the kids and deliver money to her sister for their keep. As time went on, she started coming less and less often. She sent the checks in the mail. More than once, mom said, she would get cleaned up, put on her one nice dress and wait in the yard all afternoon, sure that her mother would come. That's how I so often see her still, a hopeful, but sad little girl, sitting on the steps in her Sunday best waiting for a mother that never comes. I wonder if that's why she was always giving people things, feeling that giving only herself would never be enough. Strangely, she ended up doing the very same thing to her first two children when she married my father. Having her all to himself was always his agenda it seems. I've only seen them twice in my whole life. Her mother took them and moved to California so she could never see them, (according to my mother) – and I thought *my* life was strange.

Giving of ourselves is always enough. It is the greatest gift we have to offer. I bring all of this to the table only to encourage you to reflect for a moment upon the family life situations that leave their indelible imprints on us all. So it is too, with the cultural contexts we are born into; not to mention whatever religious indoctrination that we receive from family and culture alike. Friends and Family, God and Country, what a tangle we all too quickly find ourselves in! Small wonder the greater part of our young lives is spent in simply "trying to find the answers." A great many of us just stuff the impulse and never do. The past can be a heavy burden; sinking deep inside. I encourage you to raise it all into the light. Recognize how it all has influenced you. Then let it go.

The experiences of your life have given you a certain skill set that is unique in the world. What you perceive as your flaws may prove to be your greatest assets. Stop suffering over comparisons to what might have been. Accept what is. Accept everything you are. The fact that you're reading this reflects that you are at least exploring the possibility of a clearer, freer, way of living - Blessings to you and your success. Persistence is the key. Life is fraught with countless distractions that will dissipate your energies. Be wise. Choose your endeavors, and then learn maintain your focus. Yes, the odds are against you, but then they always have been. You've already found your way through countless trials and troubles - And you're still here. That ought to tell you something.

27.

Let Life Jump on You!

Whenever I teach, there are always a few who linger after class to share a bit of who they are. I try to do the same. I strive to be authentic, to be present for the exchange, warts and all. They quickly discover I don't have all the answers to their questions. Sometimes the answers I have are not the ones they want to hear. Sometimes what they have to say is not what I want to hear.

Our relationships with others are colored by our expectations more than we care to admit. At their source expectations mean you're referencing the past or projecting your desires upon the future. Life is about now. *This* is the future you've been waiting for. How do you like it? Is it what you expected? Do you find yourself capable of being OK with it just as it is?

How does the day, any day, compare with your expectation of it? "Have a nice day!" "Having a bad day?" What a bullshit way of living a life. How about, "There will be moments of beauty in your life today, watch for them!" or "I hope your troubles dissolve into nothing for a while today." Why color a whole day blue? Look at how many colors there are, everywhere, all of the time. It's never just black or white. Grey is not always gloomy, (it's actually one of my very favorite colors.) A few clouds between you and the Sun are inevitable. Sometimes they're welcome, sometimes not - Roll with it. Just when you think you know how it's going to go, life jumps out of the bushes – "SURPRISE!" You either laugh or have a heart attack. It's up to you.

28.

On the Road to Enlightenment

Many years ago while wandering the jungles of Southeast Asia I was given a book of Zen koans. From that point on, the possibility of spiritual enlightenment created a subtle tension within me that keeps me on my toes. It has served as the catalyst for countless joyous moments. Whenever that tension bursts forth into effortless knowing, grace is there. It has also led me on many a wild goose chase. So much of the journey has been about the shifts in what I thought "enlightenment" was.

When I was in my twenties I thought it must be like an acid trip, where everything would be like a Peter Max cartoon with "Sergeant Peppers Lonely Heart's Club Band" or "Lucy in the Sky With Diamonds" playing in the background. Ever so slowly, it eventually dawned on me that it was every day life that was the acid trip, especially in Vietnam. What I was looking for was something a little – no, make that a lot – less chaotic.

In '71, after I got back home, yoga and TM (Transcendental Meditation) helped quiet things down for a while. Yet, simultaneously I felt like a stranger in a strange land. Like so many Vets, my little trip to Vietnam changed me in ways my friends just couldn't understand. I found myself desperately in need of a little peace to balance the world of war from which I had recently returned. Just getting high didn't work very well for me anymore. Yoga was pretty "weird" in the "greaser" circles of the South Suburbs of Chicago in 1973. But I persevered, and just about that time that I started feeling centered and strong, along came an old girlfriend with LOTS of baggage and proceeded to show me just how enduring our old habit energies can be. In retrospect, there were more than a few Karmic ties in that relationship to be undone, which is often the case whenever we 'decide' a relationship is over when it's obviously not. In no time at all many of my extremely destructive, but very familiar coping mechanisms moved back in to my life and refused to leave. I was the only home they'd ever known - poor things. Predictably, the whole episode then drew painfully to a close.

Then I decided, "To hell with enlightenment! I'll just marry that sexy, blued eyed blonde at work that caught me on the rebound and buy a house and dedicate myself to settling down, having some kids and find satisfaction in living the ever-popular (and oh so elusive) American Dream." It was O.K. but it wasn't what I was looking for. My little guys brought me a lot of joy, but the rest of it felt pretty empty.

Then I thought I'd just get away from it all and join an old friend (we were in 'nam together) in a North Woods lifestyle that I was sure would be a lot more peaceful, which it was, for about 6 months – until I started working 12 hour days and still couldn't make any money; and my best friend secretly became very fond of cocaine; and we both started drinking way too much and our business went belly up; and I lost my house back in Chicago and declared bankruptcy; and discovered that my wife of 12 years was not my friend and then – I blew out my knee in a twisting fall and started eating Vicodin with every meal; and couldn't work, or drive, or even get a cup of coffee from the counter to the table without spilling it all over and I was totally freaking out; and then - something very strange happened.

In a little college town on the Southern shore of Lake Bemidji, in Northern Minnesota, (pop. 10,000) where according to the *Bemidji Pioneer* newspaper, many of my Northwoods neighbors thought Pat Robertson would make a fine President – I learned Tai Chi Chih from a beautiful woman who wore rings on her toes, and flowers in her hair - And *that* changed everything.

29.

Peace and Quiet

Life in modern America is a noisy affair. I deeply relish that time during classes when we sit or stand together, unspeaking, unmoving, in silent stillness. Usually, when the body is moving it is being driven by a noise in the head. Thoughts are such noisy things; always in motion; burning energy; stealing attention. It's as if they're attuned to all the noise we encounter in our daily combustion engined, automobiled, electrically humming, tv'd, computered, I-pod, camera phoned, consumption driven version of the good life; while scrambling daily to pay all the monthly's here in the greatest country on earth; and are compelled to add to the din ...or is it the other way around? Aha! So *that's* where all this noise is coming from!

Qigong is the only movement I know that creates stillness. What a strange thing. How wonderful. I once read that there is nothing so much like the voice of God as silence. Any time I have ever felt deep peace and contentment, silence and stillness were there. I'd be willing to bet it is the same with you.

Silence is so little sought after in the modern world. There's so much noise and business going on that introducing a little quiet and stillness to such a busy mind and body might feel downright uncomfortable. I'll admit it takes some getting used to. Who would ever guess that it's what they've been looking for. It's so easy to miss. If it feels like nothing at all it's because nothing is exactly what it is. It's that nothing from which you and I and our whole noisy, chaotic world arise. It's where we come from. That quiet, empty space in which everything arises is home.

I remember a talk I attended back in 1973, given by Maharishi Mahesh Yogi where he talked a bit about levitation. "It's considered a miracle," he said. "But all we have to do is go about 65 miles that way," he went on, pointing straight up, "and *everything* is floating!" I closed my eyes and tried to envision a hundred billion worlds, whirling around a hundred billion stars, some being born, some dying; a hundred billion galaxies, all floating in a vast emptiness, quiet and still. And I somehow felt myself as that vast quiet stillness.

That simple statement so many years ago fired my imagination and set me on a collision course with nothingness. It inspires me still. Nothingness, its nature is beyond grasping, but not beyond knowing. Just because you can't describe it, doesn't mean it isn't there. You *can* know it. Become empty, quiet, and still, and you *will* know it. A little practice can help that happen. It leads you home.

30.

It's Not What You Think

I've been a practitioner of the Art & science of Qigong for over two decades. I can't understand why even seasoned practitioners have such limiting attitudes concerning it. For instance, why is qigong considered primarily a medical protocol by so many? Is this deep connection to Source that arises during practice supposed to be a secret? There's no denying that it is a powerful tool for optimizing proper physical function. In my case that has most certainly been true.

First it healed my torn and tattered knee. Then it went on to reveal that my tendency to self-medicate my anxiety and stress with alcohol (moderately but regularly applied,) was contributing to that very stress and anxiety. Once I quit drinking I found my gastric problems rapidly improving. Indigestion and irregularity all but disappeared in just a few short weeks. A feeling of well-being began to dominate my days. I slept better. I ate better. Binge eating was one of the reasons I've gained and lost and gained back hundreds of pounds in my life. My weight stabilized. After learning and practicing Steven Ridley's *Harmony Qigong* for just a few months, the crippling migraine headaches that had made so many days of my life a living hell went away and never came back.

In that regard, life in general has been kind to me in comparison to other members of my family. Both my mother and father had their first heart attacks in their fifties. Both she and my father had high blood pressure, subsequent heart attacks and adult onset diabetes. My father suffered from debilitating headaches that occurred every month or so through his entire life. My younger siblings haven't faired much better. My younger brother has been hospitalized with bleeding ulcers and my sister struggles with liver disease. Both have had life threatening bouts with cancer. Another brother died from a drug overdose while still in his thirties. Drugs are never the appropriate answer to the challenges of life. The baby of the family moved to Las Vegas and hasn't been heard from since he left his wife and stepdaughter years ago. Life's been hard on the Nielsen clan. Somehow I've come through it all rather well. I'm healthier and happier than I've ever been. I feel physically strong, mentally and emotionally well-balanced, constantly aware of a higher presence (call it what you will) and creative endeavors spontaneously arise and bring great joy in their process and execution. Sobriety is no longer a struggle. I've come to enjoy the deep satisfaction in facing all that life brings my way head on. I'm convinced that all of these blessings are primarily a result of my Qigong practice.

I've heard that one can achieve greater health, heightened awareness and mental clarity as a result of eating this and drinking that, but have never been much of a fan. I love cake and cookies and ice cream and candy and cheeseburgers and pasta and diet soda. I have been known to drive miles to investigate someone's claim that they have discovered a place that makes "The best chocolate malt in the world." I think I would rather be dead than macrobiotic. I just make sure I eat my veggies and munch on fruit and drink enough water too - So far, so good.

Personally, as far as diet is concerned, I think we humans are two-legged coyotes. We can eat just about anything and flourish.. We're omnivores (and predators) like bears and wolves. We're scavengers and opportunists. It's how we're made. It's part of the reason we're overrunning the planet. We're easily one of the most adaptable creatures alive. When it comes to diet don't get crazy. Everything in moderation and you're likely to be just fine.

I'll be the first to admit that the physical manifestations of Qigong practice are wonderful. When the body feels good, I feel good. I'm also convinced that I am not my body. It's a rental. I've got a license to cruise around in it for a while, and I'm absolutely thrilled that it's one of those high mileage low maintenance designs.

Yes, there are those who would argue – "no body, no experience!" On one level they may have a point, but that particular point of view would also state, "I am not empty space," (really?), "I am solid matter" and offer themselves to your touch to prove it. "No brain, no consciousness!" (again - really?). Is a thought a thing? A feeling? An Aha! moment? What can we make of all those near death experiences that have emerged as technology has literally brought people back from the brink, and even though they were 'gone' reported all that they saw and heard while they were clinically dead?

The truth is we live not just in the world, but in many worlds at once, a multi–dimensional composite. There isn't just one reality. Reality is not so much 'the way things are' as a process of endless unfolding: bodies, brains, stars, worlds, feelings, life, all emerging from a single Source. What an amazing thing.

Qigong too is a process. It is a way of embracing and becoming a conscious active participant in this great and mysterious dance of Yin and Yang. It is so much more than healing hurts and renewing and restoring damaged or malfunctioning body parts. It is most importantly a very reliable way of gaining insight into the truth of what's really going on.

31.

A History Lesson

Like so many culture-specific practices that have arrived upon the world stage as the age of information continues to unfold, even in its culture of origin Qigong's history is shrouded in mystery, and it's countless practitioners (and *their* revelations) are lost in the mists of time. I often find myself wondering, who were these guys?

The free thinkers and non-participants in any greater culture always find themselves marginalized, and for good reason. The founders of any of the great religions of the world were inevitably branded heretics and blasphemers in their day. Even in our modern world every new scientific discovery must run the gauntlet of the powers that be. There are always those who weigh themselves solely upon the scales of some established institution. and respond to any intrusion upon their 'hallowed halls' as vehemently as a physical attack upon their person. Any affront to those proclivities that have brought with them power, prestige and political influence are frequently dealt with as harshly as attempted murder, rather than simply being seen as an endorsement of a new and different idea. More than a few untimely deaths can be blamed on standing undaunted in the light of truth. The scattered ruins of lives and reputations litter the hallowed halls of science, as well as those of history and religion.

That being said, it is not surprising that the schools of thought that give rise to such men have been secret out of necessity. Free thinkers, a natural result of self-inquiry, have always been a thorn in the side of any established institution of knowledge. The pursuit of knowledge is far too often the pursuit of power, influence, and prestige (all egoic tendencies) than any real desire to know the truth.

So it should come as no surprise that any expounded self-revelation (read-new idea) arising in the midst of a culture's established institutions (read-orthodox view) can turn very quickly into all kinds of marvelously creative unpleasantness for the representatives of truth. Fundamentalists posing as men of knowledge are the most dangerous animals on earth. The realization of any truth born of "the kingdom within" is far too often going to clash (sometimes violently) with the established kingdoms without.

Yet, before they become institutionalized, the greatest philosophies; the greatest discoveries; the greatest human progress, social or scientific, always erupt mysteriously into the physical world from the realm of the unseen – the realm of spirit. The powers established in the world resent and resist its intrusion every time. It is one of human society's most disturbing traits. Perhaps violence is a required condition of creation after all.

I believe that it was Mircea Eliade in *The Myth of the Eternal Return*, who said:

> *By far the most common way men have of dealing with phenomena so novel that it calls for a major reorganization of their preconceptions, is to ignore them altogether, or persecute those who bear witness to them.*

The Qigong practitioners of old knew this and acted accordingly. If you have an inclination to preserve a tradition, that would be a fine one to keep in mind.

32.

Self Inquiry

The first day of a beginner's class always excites me. All of those new faces are not necessarily expressing the quiet serenity that I've grown used to in those students who've been practicing awhile. There's considerably more evidence of worry, anxiety and stress written there. I'm excited because I know that's about to change. Qigong always delivers. It is a foundation upon which we can build a richer, healthier life. Aside from saving you a ton of money on medical bills, Qigong contributes greatly toward healing matters of the head and heart as well.

Instead of spending years in psychotherapy and its neck deep foray into your own personal pile of garbage, why not just learn to let it go? Of course it's very satisfying to talk about you, you, you, but that 'you' thing is the problem, not the solution. You're simply trading an old me, for a new me, and it's the 'me' that is the problem!

So, dad didn't like you. Does that mean you are unlikeable? You say you can't do anything right? You're still here aren't you? A lot of people aren't. You're always making mistakes? How else does anyone learn anything? "Sometimes I'm so… so… Yin!" Yes. Yes you are. "Then I'm so Yang!" Yes. Yes, that's true too. What you're looking for is balance.

You see, you aren't inherently any way at all (except alive!). Everything else is arbitrary. Quit wallowing in opinions of yourself. They don't mean very much. The only power they have is the power you give them. Stop insisting that you need to be what you think you should be. A little self-inquiry is in order… Why do you think there's a certain something you need to be or do? What's in it for you? What's the payoff? Where is this stuff coming from?

I recently had a new student come up to me after class and say, "I feel like I've been hypnotized."

"I think you've got it backwards," I said. "You *were* hypnotized and now you're not. Do you feel anxious or uncomfortable?"

"No," she answered.

"How do you feel?

"Peaceful. Quiet."

That's how clarity feels. It's what spontaneously arises when we are no longer caught in the cycle of thought → creating feeling → creating thought → creating feeling and see the process a little more objectively for what it is -

33.

A Mayan View of Time

I have recently come across a fascinating exposition of how the ancient Mayans viewed time. It involves the mystery of the Mayan Calendar. According to Carl Johan Calleman in his book, *The Mayan Calendar and the Transformation of Consciousness*, the reason that there is an end to the Mayan way of measuring time is that through each of 9 great cycles (called underworlds) each containing 13 heavens (each comprised of a figurative 7 days and 6 nights) there is a natural expansion and contraction of conscious energy (How about that; an actual living, *breathing* universe!) There is a natural acceleration of occurrences within each cycle, as well as a contraction of time in each subsequent cycle. The whole structure rather resembles an inverted pyramid, which ends at a single point in time in December of the year 2012. It's a whole new twist on Einstein's theory of time being relative. Only this time it's relative to the transformation of consciousness in the physical world.

To clarify any confusion, let's say in one cycle it took a million years for things to evolve to a certain point. (The calendar actually indicates it started about 16,400 million years ago, but let's not get lost in the details.) During the next cycle, that same amount of evolution would happen twenty times faster (50,000 yrs.). In this way creation would be constantly gaining momentum. During the next cycle things would happen twenty times faster than that (2500 yrs.) and so on, and so on, until things were happening so fast you could hardly keep track! Guess where we are? Yep, this is the point in the cycle when it's all happening so fast that it makes your head spin. Can you feel it? According to the Maya, we're at the end of 16.4 billion years of constant evolution to a point where everything that can happen is all happening at once. We're living in the last 13 years of the ever accelerating movement of time. 1999 to 2012 is the final cycle, the coming to fruition of all that has been.

Quite the concept, eh? I have to admit to a bit of excitement as I entertain the notion. It certainly would explain a lot of things. I try to be open, living with questions instead of searching for answers, but I guess we'll know soon enough. Wouldn't it be something if it proved to be true? – The end of history.

The progression of the last hundred years or so does seem mind-boggling. Great Grandma Nelson (my wife's maiden name) used to tell the story of how her father sent one of her first suitors packing when he showed up in a horse and buggy with a fancy fringe on top. Her father wouldn't let her out of the house. "A boy with a fringe top buggy has just one thing on his mind," he said. Before she died at the age of 96, she would see people flying in jumbo jets at 500 mph and men walking on the moon. That's some serious acceleration!

Reading Plato or Marcus Aurelius one clearly sees that it isn't because were so much wiser or smarter than men a couple of thousand years ago. How did we manage to come so far, so fast? The Maya may have the answer.

If it's true, what of personal growth, could a reasonable effort today produce twenty times the benefit of an even greater effort a couple of thousand years ago? Is "enlightened" living suddenly within our grasp? I have the feeling it had better be.

I don't agree with the apocalyptic traditions that an end is near or that some great cataclysm is about to be played out without even a Noah or an ark this time around, but an end is an end. It is much more likely that things will continue on, but in a different way. The world we know will end and a new one will be born of a new way of knowing, a new way of seeing. I can't help but think that grace, as always, will get us through.

Richard Dawkins brings to light a wonderful moment in his book *The God Delusion:*

> *"Tell me, the great twentieth century philosopher Ludwig Wittgenstein once asked a friend, "Why do people always say it was natural for man to assume that the sun went round the Earth rather than that the Earth was rotating?"*

His friend replied, "Well, obviously because it just looks as though the sun is going round the Earth!"

Wittgenstein responded, "Well what would it have looked like if it had looked as though the Earth was rotating?"

I think the "end" will be more like that.

The real mind blower about the Mayan Calendar is that it is not just a way of measuring time. It is literally a map recording the transformation of consciousness through time. This from a culture in the jungles of Central America that was at it's height over a thousand years ago! That shines a rather glaring light on our somewhat limited view of Western history don't you think? Ah, but there's more…

The Mayans believed that at the center of all of creation there was a Central Sun that could not be seen. They called it Hun Ahau, literally, the "One lord." Their symbol for it looked like this:

34.

From Rudolph Steiner's *How to Know Higher Worlds:*

"Our civilization is more inclined to criticize, judge, and condemn than to feel devotion and selfless veneration ...But just as surely as every feeling of devotion and reverence nurtures the soul's powers for higher knowledge, so every act of criticism and judgment drives these powers away. Reverence, awe, adoration, and wonder are replaced by other feelings.

Each moment that we spend becoming aware of whatever derogatory, judgmental, and critical opinions still remain in our consciousness brings us closer to higher knowledge. We advance even more quickly if in such moments, we fill our consciousness with admiration, respect and reverence for the world and life ... such moments awaken forces in us that otherwise remain dormant.

What food is to the body, feelings are to the soul. If we feed the body stones instead of bread, it will cease to function. (So it is with the soul. We must nourish it with reverence, respect, and devotion.)"

We must develop the skill to recognize the divine aspects of ourselves within before we will be able to find the divine in our surroundings. This is what I call practicing "Enlightened Self-Interest," learning that we *are* the world, the inner and outer aspect being the same. What we see within is what we see without. It cannot be any other way.

35.

Anchor Deep

The outer forces of life can only press in upon you when you allow it to happen. Like a tree trying to grow in a cleft in the rock, you're likely to feel like you're barely hanging on. You're going to feel like you don't have all you need to support you.

On the other hand, you can choose to cultivate your own space in which to grow, where the roots of your life can anchor deep and access all you need from the Source of Life that created you. How different that life feels.

Each day remove yourself from the grinding wheel of the world and into the stream that drives the wheel; the current flowing clear and strong far removed from the purposes of the mass of men; that wellspring of endless supply.

The price of admission: Relaxing into stillness.

36.

Some Days You're the Pigeon, Some Days the Statue

Where do you look to determine what you want from life? Do you want what your parents had? Do you look to those around you and align yourself with what others determine has worth? We all did that a lot, in seventh grade. And anyway, who wants to stand out, except maybe Paris Hilton? So how do you determine what will bring happiness, joy, fulfillment?

The best and wisest teachers have all instructed us that the answer lies within. I don't know about your "within" but mine is a landfill. I should clarify that. The thinking, judging, trip down memory lane part feels like a city dump overflowing with all kinds of garbage. Curiously, everything there is something I once thought I needed to help define who and what I was.

Linus's blanket takes many forms. Lucy's psychotherapy really is worth about 5¢. And you have to remember that she will always pull the football out of the way at the last minute. She can't help it. You have to know that. One-ups-man-ship in the world of human endeavor is going to be, more often than not, the rule of the day. Some days you're the port-a-potty, some days you're the blue deodorant thingy. Excuse me for a moment would you? I think I'm going to go do a little Qigong.

Ahhh, much better...

Speaking of little deodorant thingies, do you remember the Port-A-Potty guy in the *Woodstock* movie? What a wonderful human being. I couldn't begin to count how many times I have thought of him over the years as a powerful symbol of being at peace with what is. I wonder if he knew what a fine Zen teacher he was!

37.

Lighten Up

We each have certain talents and abilities that we effortlessly express. We also have many more that exist but lie dormant or undeveloped within. The depth and degree of human potential is grossly underestimated simply because we rarely take the time or find the means on an individual basis to express so much more than we do. It sounds like a lot of work. For such an anxious animal learning to relax sure feels like work. Part of it is we simply don't *believe* that we can effortlessly accomplish purposes more in alignment with our natural abilities. You just *think* it's going to be harder than it is. It's got nothing to do with thinking, and everything to do with feeling.

Relax! It's a lot more work constantly trying to conform to your perceived notions of what you *should* do. Quit trying to make the world the way you want it. *That's* what isn't going to work! You've got to lighten up.

Your self image is for the most part a hodgepodge of past experiences pasted together in memory that eventually becomes a very limited definition of what your capacities are. You've also been influenced by family, friends, and culture, your whole life. The discovery of the unfathomable depth of you becomes increasingly unlikely as you express your unconscious conclusions, live accordingly, and close the book on the matter.

Reopen the book. Let an ever grander story unfold. Life then becomes one of those books you just can't put down, full of shocks and surprises, one that grabs you and won't let go. "A real page turner!" " The best story ever!"

"Use it or lose it" is nature's way. "If you need it, I'll create it" is also its way. That self image you carry is its subtle manifestation. Bring in more energy, bring in more awareness and new "discoveries" are the inevitable result. Evolution has supplied you with the hardware for greater consciousness; the software is up to you.

With the bright, noisy, world tugging at you constantly, you react with the program your computer came with. It rests with you to discover when all the information coming in isn't being processed in a way deeply meaningful to you and change the program. You don't have to settle. Tweak it to your liking. You say you're O.K. with the way things are? Ask yourself, is your satisfaction rooted in deep understanding or is it just what you've grown accustomed to?

The source and ground of deep understanding is stillness. It is a field of pure potential, clear and unadulterated, to which are added all things that arise within it. It is invisible. You can't see it, touch it, taste it, smell or hear it. But it is there. You can learn to feel it. To truly know it you must become it. There really is no other way.

To accomplish this you have to give up…cut loose from…cease to identify with…what you thought you were. It takes faith. It takes courage. It takes persistence. But it can be done. Just a little effort every day will help you to relax into it. It's tough letting go, but it's the only way to be truly free.

This universal love of freedom so prevalent in humanity is Life's subtle coaxing in the direction of our highest good. It is this innate impulse toward unlimited possibility that leads us ever out and away from all that we think we know, so that we may someday discover (or perhaps rediscover) our true place in the order of things, and as has been said – see it clearly for the very first time.

38.

In Gratitude

There are times after a good move with competent students that I'm literally flying. There is such deep joy in the Qigong state. How does one speak of such things? There are no words. I want to hug everyone, as if that would somehow communicate to them what is welling up inside from the Source inexhaustible. I've noticed that when Qi is flowing powerfully I often have the urge to physically touch others as I talk with them. In quiet hope that in doing so the person with whom I'm speaking will somehow share in this wonder coursing through me. It feels prompted by the life force itself that cannot, will not, be contained.

Once it begins to flow it pours into the world through me. How can I stay open enough not to lose it? How can I stay open enough to realize it can't be lost? I try not to touch it with the mind or emotions and simply allow it continue to develop and evolve within me.

As it flows through me I am blessed. I feel a deep and abiding gratitude. I have joined the masters and practitioners of this artful science who have opened themselves through the centuries to become willing conduits of this miracle of Qi. The countless generations who have practiced and taught and shared with whoever wanted to learn, this sweet, nourishing, mystery of Qigong. You are my brothers. You are my teachers. You are the carriers of a sacred trust without which my life would feel so much less than the miracle it is.

39.

Short and Sweet

The truth is not something to be searched for it is something to be present for. It is all that is. There is no other.

As Joan Tollifson says in *Awake in the Heartland:*

I am the space in which it all unfolds in a single timeless instant...when we see what is as God – IT IS GOD – that's the mystery ... that's the alchemy. It's all in the seeing.

40.

A Koan

The Qigong state is an ever - reliable reference point. An infallible guide beyond the duality of Mind and thinking mind that reveals thinking for what it is – something we have to leave behind in order to truly "know." Thinking mind is everlasting argument. You will find no peace there, only endless antagonism. Thinking mind is Hell. 'Peace of mind' an oxymoron. 'Peace of Mind' beyond mind – now you've got potential! Do you see it?

41.

Simplicity

The power of Qigong lies in its simplicity. Like enlightenment, it is an open secret. You do what you always do – you move, you watch, you breathe. You just do it with awareness. You do it with intent. You do it with power, but a different kind of power. You do not seek to overwhelm, conquer or subdue. It is not forced, you simply focus on what you intend to do and then you do it.

At first, perhaps not so well, so you practice. You get better, and you practice some more. Every day you improve. In time, you accomplish effortlessly what you intend. In time, the secret is revealed – you are intention; you are awareness, you are breath and body – all at once. It is the awareness of the "all at once" part that is the essence of your power; your consciousness, the source of all that is. Like all true things, it's really quite simple.

42.

On Righteousness

Most people try to be this, and not that, to be good, not bad; right, not wrong; strong, not weak. I'm here to tell you it can't be done. Any resistance to completeness is dealt with very harshly by that wholeness of which it is a part. Any separation is an illusion only, a trick of the thinking, structuring mind, a self-delusion. To say, I am this, and not that, is the gravest of errors. Creation will not let it stand for long. In the realm of the physical whatever stands in the light creates a shadow. Whatever has a front must have a back. Yin cannot exist without Yang and vice versa. Each defines the other. Each is the source of the other's becoming. The truth contains *all* things.

And so, you may find yourself becoming what you swore you were not. Saying and doing what you despise in others. Know this is inevitable and live lightly, without judging things. Trying to entrench oneself in righteousness is a sure road to disaster. What is more, it will cause you to lose faith in your Self, and that is not easily undone.

43.

The Subtlety of Words

A Zen master named Bankei (1622-1693) was eulogized by a blind man: "Since I cannot see a person's face, I must judge his sincerity by his voice. Usually when I hear someone congratulate a friend on some success, I also hear envy in his voice, and when I hear expressions of condolence, I often hear a secret tone of pleasure. Not so with Bankei; when he expressed happiness his voice was completely happy, and when he expressed sadness, sadness was all I heard."

Some of the meanings I hear when people use the word – God:

A) All that is (makes me want to hug them)
B) My God, not yours. (Ouch!)
C) Christ not Allah. (Or vice versa – I'm right you're wrong)
D) The one I follow that wants me to… (Scares me a little)
E) A belief I hold that, should you not agree, I will use to justify my being cruel, mocking or apathetic toward you and your children. (Makes me sad)
F) The one I follow that makes me better than you (makes me sadder still)

For me, God is Love: The seeing of all things as your Self. There is nothing God is not. There is nothing you are not. There is no separation. No "other". How different the world would be if each one of us instead of 'swearing to God' would simply swear to Love - everything, everyone - the whole play of consciousness – this ever-changing dance of light and shadows.

44.

The Cathedral of Mind

The interesting thing about problems is that they never seem to be solved on the level in which they're occurring. For instance if I need more money to live the way I want, the solution could be figuring out a way to make more money. That is more another problem than a solution. Or I can change my mind about what I want. Or…begin an inquiry as to why I want it.

A solution to my not having enough money may lead to an awareness of how I'm spending it a little too frivolously. A realization that I never have enough of anything arises. I may discover a fundamental sense of lack that I try to fill with "stuff". Can it be filled? Should it be filled? What is it about those empty spaces within us that make us uncomfortable? Is that all we are: stuff piled on stuff piled on stuff? What's wrong with empty except there's nothing there. If there is no empty, there is no room for anything new, for anything more. Yet it is through our constant wanting that we begin to discover how incredibly vast this emptiness within truly is. The realization that it will never be filled is a starting point for revelation.

As far as filling empty spaces, we must take our lessons from the universe itself. When it comes to "stuff" a little goes a long way. How little matter there is in the vastness of creation. Where too much exists chaos reigns. Great emptiness is required for nature's purposes to unfold – within and without. Let emptiness be. Quit filling it. Start throwing stuff out. You don't' need it.

How beautiful, a single rose in an empty room. How wonderful to be contained within a great cathedral looming vaulted and gilded, high and empty overhead. In such a space we are easily moved to sense the wonder of emptiness.

In times past it was the vault of heaven that evoked awe and wonder; then came a time of great halls and cathedrals as man thought to capture some essence of God's vast and intricate creation within towering vaulted spaces. All of our creations are attempted expressions of the vastness we sense within.

The question is, can we truly come to know *through experience* that all is contained in the miracle that we are? I say the answer is a resounding, Yes! The challenge is to quit seeing ourselves as merely this or that. We are the reflection of all that is. All that has ever been is contained within us. There is nothing that we are not. There should be no separation, no divorce imposed upon us by this appearance of mind. Mind cannot contain it any more than the greatest of cathedrals. That's the truth. Know it. Embrace it. Embody it, and as has been said, the truth of it may indeed set us free.

45.

Safe Harbor

It's a scary proposition to willingly cut your self loose from familiar moorings and trust in the powerful currents of Life seeking expression. Yet, if you're truly honest about it, have you ever been in control? Should the storms of Life find you tied to the pier – you're doomed. Safe harbor is anything but. A gentle swell in the deep becomes a shattering wave in the shallows. Don't be so anxious to set an anchor. Imagined securities, familiar patterns, comforting routines, all can disappear in an instant. Just because you don't know where you are, doesn't mean you're lost. There is a wisdom in life's unpredictable currents, learn to trust them. You are buoyant and free. You are meant for the open sea. Ride out life's storms away from any safe haven. For in truth, there are none.

46.

I Am Not a Buddhist

At the heart of the Diamond Sutra of Buddhism lies the statement "Let your Mind come forth without fixing it anywhere." It expresses beautifully the essence of one of the primary goals of the faith – non-attachment.

Mind is sticky. It wants to attach itself to anything that comes into its field of awareness. It's a free floating dream that wants to become something, anything - everything. It's perfectly natural and yet there is also a quiet desperation in it. It wants to attach a "self" to things; to find a definition it can rest upon; to say I am this and this and that and that; OR I like this and not that, this has value that does not. This is bad that is good; mind is prone to identify with either Yin or Yang. Not both. It defines through separation and negation.

Mind is simply following the impulse of life to expand and grow in countless directions to become everything. It is the way of creation. The trick is to avoid getting stuck to any of its manifestations and missing out on the rest. Yes, it's all dream stuff. Yes, it's really happening, and yes you are a part of it. To see it as process, not personality, is the challenge. It's not personal. It's the play of consciousness that you see. Play is what it does. A dance of light and shadows

As I practice moving softly, breathing easily, simply watching… watching… mind becomes less sticky. So much to watch, so much to feel, no time in which to judge, pick, choose. In such a moment there is peace & joy; a sweet moment's relief from relentless mental chatter; immersed in the stillness that emerges when mind is not fixed anywhere. Yet, I am not a Buddhist. I take my lessons where I find them. And I find them often as I relax, breathe, and feel my way through form. What a simple way to clear away the clutter that obscures the truth of things.

47.

The Many Ways of Knowing

There is no more reliable way of truly knowing something than to embody it. Whenever we choose to give mental, emotional energy a conscious means of expression through physical embodiment it becomes a way of knowing.

Whether it's swimming, golf, bowling or Qigong, the body becomes the instrument, the field of endeavor, the song. It is the process of all becoming. Consciously developing greater skill in the focusing of our intent toward any endeavor automatically brings joy. The degree to which our nature is aligned with our particular endeavor (talent), determines the level of joy experienced. Horses love to run, squirrels love to climb, badgers love to dig. Mankind loves to know. It's our blessing and our curse. "Knowing" is the source of our greatest joy. Thinking we know and defending it, even with our lives - our greatest curse. It is our woeful "missing of the mark" (sin).

> *Making a self out of our knowing, inevitably leads to our undoing.*
> *"Those who the Gods would destroy, they first make proud."*

True humility is nothing more than being satisfied through becoming more and more aware of this ever unfolding process of greater and greater knowing. True knowing is not the endless accumulation and assimilation of information; it is becoming aware of what was always there and making it conscious. It is what the universe is doing.

The light of Yang is ever present in the heart of Yin; the shadow of Yin the unavoidable result of Yang unfolding as the world. We look to the night sky and resting in earth's shadow we see only dark. Yet, the light of the moon is not of the moon, and the dark of night is but a shadow of the earth itself, basking in the greater light in which it resides. Let those who have eyes see. Sharpen your vision. It just takes a little practice.

Begin with your intention. Little by little, strengthen your resolve. Your endeavor will come to fruition through the offering of your body and your breath to something greater. Wisdom would dictate that your highest good is best served by doing all you can to align with life's joyous purpose. It's not as hard as you think. You have to breathe and move anyway. Why not do it with great skill?

"If one is master of one thing and understands one thing well, one has at the same time, insight into and understanding of many things".

~Vincent Van Gogh

48.

Know What's Gotta Go

What if the scale on which you weigh yourself gave you a reading based on an arbitrary condition. I mean, what if it didn't start from zero, but started from the last reading it gave and went up from there? Do you think you'd notice? Would there be a moment of – "Oh…my…God!!" Or simply "Wait a minute…that can't be right." So you step on again and now it's even higher. Now you know something is up. The scale is useless. Now you have no way of measuring how "heavy" you've become, at least until you find a way of recalibrating the instrument to zero.

So you look in the mirror instead. Your baseline becomes that image in the mirror. What about thoughts? How do they affect what you see? How about the emotional condition (mood) coloring those thoughts? Which has the greater impact on what you experience what you see, what you feel, or what you think? Do you see the problem? *Every* dimension of your being adds its weight to your perception of what you are. Take some time each day to recalibrate the instrument to zero. It's the easiest way to lose the weight you've accumulated that I know.

At a certain level of being "too heavy" you are going to have to lighten up or continue to live with the limitations brought about by all the crap that has somehow become a part of you.

You can do it! It's your road to greater freedom of thought, experience, and action. Just like cleaning out the garage is the way to have space enough for your car. You're getting your priorities in order. Once you get started tossing things out, you'll probably begin to wonder just when it was that you began to think you actually needed all that stuff.

Tossing out old conditioned responses, well-worn mental loops, and outdated self-imaging is as simple as just not giving them your attention anymore. Warning! - Don't start getting sentimental. They gotta' go! It's the first step toward gaining a little more inner space. The emptier you are, the more clarity you'll have. You won't be as likely to get bogged down. You've got to travel light. Nobody enjoys the feeling that life is passing them by. But, when every nook and cranny of you is packed with mementos of the past, how exciting can the ride really be?

49.

Just Another Day in Paradise

I am absolutely amazed how much happens in any single day. Since I woke up this morning I've already experienced being drowsy, anxious, hungry, confused, agitated, satisfied, compassionate, caring, altruistic, responsible, generous, loving, selfish, impatient, disciplined, reflective, Self-absorbed and peaceful.

I've brushed my teeth, washed my face, combed my hair, made my wife a cup of tea, said a prayer, gotten dressed, made the bed, ate a muffin, fed the cat, fed the rabbit, read a bit, washed my face, combed my hair, practiced Qigong, spent a few minutes sitting in stillness, and wrote it all down. I woke up at 8:00 a.m. and it's only twenty minutes after nine.

Wow!

What a ride!

Sixteen hours to go!...

50.

Let's be Honest

In the course of any day or for that matter any moment, we humans are as tuned in to our immediate surroundings or situations as a police scanner is to one specific frequency. We're all over the place. One moment we're rolling down the road lost in a thought stream; the next we're slamming on the brakes and cursing the guy in front of us for forcing us out of it. Then we're angry at him because we didn't get enough sleep last night because of the kids. Then we're angry at the kids. Then we take a sip of coffee and feel a little better and reflect for a moment how much we like Sumatra roast and Starbucks and start feeling a little guilty about all those poor Guatemalans who get paid squat for their beans and as we roll into work, about how we love or hate our job, or our boss, or our co-workers and how now we have to pee… And it goes on like that every waking hour of the day, day after day. No wonder the #1 complaint doctors hear is "I'm just so tired all of the time!"

This is life with undisciplined mind. Instead of being on 'standby' it's full on *all the time*. Considering that it is the norm rather than the exception, is it any wonder that the world (the human world) seems mad? It is!! In the midst of all this incessant mental noise with each thoughts' emotional echo adding to the chaos within, is real communication between us; or clear thinking even possible?

You ask a question about how I'm doing today. Are you ready for a real answer? Have you got a couple of hours? So, I say, "fine, and you?" and you say "Fine, thanks," and this is normal! Yes, I understand it's a social convention, but that's not what the mind takes from it. "He's fine, she's fine. How come I'm not fine? He's happy, she's happy, how come I'm not happy? I can't help but think that a little less social convention and a little more honesty would really improve the situation. How about a new social convention? Whenever anyone asks, "How are you?" you have to respond with your dominant true thought or feeling. It doesn't have to be a long drawn out commiserating session, (that would be counter-productive), just a straight forward and honest exchange. Then, the person asking has to respond with their honest experience of that thought or feeling. Then, you say "Thank you." (No matter what they said), to honor their honesty and they say "You're welcome," to honor yours, and you're done. It might go like this:

How ya' doin'?

I'm not even at work yet and I'm already thinking about how much I hate my job.

I hate my job too, that's why go home and drink every night.

Thank you!

You're welcome!

Or like this:

How are you?

I'm worried about not having enough money.

Me too, and I make over $100,000 a year!

Thank You!

You're Welcome!

At least we'd give each other a handle on what we were experiencing. At least our minds would be dealing with the truth.

I once read that most people will say they just want to be happy. But they don't just want to be happy; they want to be happier than other people. And the problem is, they perceive other people being happier than they really are. Sounds right to me…

51.

Open and Allow

Intimacy is a primal human need. I have never met anyone who did not want it. Even those who seem to be intent on avoiding it are not immune to its pull. Intimacy is love's call. To see the other as one's self is the door through which a world of wonders awaits.

This tendency of the individual to expand beyond separateness is the part of our nature that gives me hope for humanity. It's also the place where friction is most likely to arise. However friction is not necessarily a bad thing. Friction creates heat. Sparks fly. It's exciting. It is where elements of separation come into contact to create something new.

Tension is a bit more subtle, a little less pronounced. It's an influence of pressure, an insistent inclination toward the path of least resistance.

Both are neither good nor bad. They are simply points of stress creating enough of a ruckus to capture out attention. Whether they are manifesting physically, mentally, emotionally, or spiritually, sparks fly, pressures build. They are the stuff of transformation. They subtly (or not so subtly) set your course. Attend them with wisdom.

If the wheel is squeaking – grease it.

If a mental position is too rigid – change it.

If an emotion is insistent- don't suppress it (or act on it) – feel where it's coming from.

The heart of Qigong is to "Open and allow." Because we are traveling such a wide and varied terrain we must be vigilant. A million years ago we were already programmed to investigate our environment for the source of that feeling that something was out of place. We had to investigate, looking for portents and signs. Creating a mental vision of what we could not see. Our survival depended on it.

Just like fear, those frictions and tensions are guides, nothing more. They are prompts to investigate; become intimate with such goings on. Qigong is an internal art, an invaluable tool in becoming familiar with your internal landscape. Know your territory. All that you need to know of who and what you are, and why you feel that way, can be found there – and nowhere else. Be bold. Step into the dragon's cave. The treasure that it guards belongs to you.

52.

Awakening Your Subtle Senses

I find it curious that the martial art of T'ai Chi (taiji) is so well known and Qigong is not, Qigong being taiji's great grand daddy and all. I'm happy to see that at least modern definitions are allowing such amalgamations as T'ai Chi Qigong to segue understanding in the right direction. Tai Chi too often gets lumped in with all of the other martial arts now available in one form or another, in just about every city and town in America.

I'm not surprised that there are more people seduced by the possibility of kicking ass than finding inner peace. Envisioning kicking ass is *so* satisfying! If only the kick ass crowd would wake up and realize the motivation for both is the same. Truth be told, we're tired of being afraid all the time, but which of the two is actually useful? We're not in high school any more and real life violence isn't a movie where you get punched and kicked and later that night reap the hero's reward for being so irresistibly alpha. In the physical world, teeth shatter, bones break. That awesome Steven Segal move will cripple a man for life. Even if you win, you lose. The bad guy is probably a good guy having a bad day, and you just made it a whole lot worse by hurting him really bad. How are you going to feel about that? Many say martial arts are for learning discipline and getting into shape, but they're also about learning how to hurt people. This is not a good thing. There are easier ways to walk fearlessly through the world.

The art and science of Qigong is one of the best (and fastest) ways of developing the proper relationship to fear. Fear is more than a survival instinct. Greed, envy, hatred, worry, anxiety, anger, they're all forms of fear. Fear is essentially an alarm; a signal to be alert; a moment of heightened awareness. It is nature's very insistent call to pay very close attention to what's happening. It is not necessarily a call to action. It is a call to connect with a deeper part of your self. To see it in this light requires a bit of training. It requires a point of view that transcends your animal nature (instinct) in that moment of heightened awareness (and a bit of belly breathing) and evokes an intelligent response from Source.

The ability to trigger a "default" response to fear must be cultivated. Like a spider in a web you have to discern between countless random vibrations and those that are relevant as a call to action. Learning to be still is essential. Stillness and relaxation create the proper background upon which such subtleties can be seen as they arise in the pure field of limitless possibilities and become real potential choices. Then you get to consciously choose the most appropriate life-affirming response instead of thoughtlessly reacting.

That intelligence of which you are an expression knows the appropriate response. Your responsibility lies in letting it arise and noticing it when it does. This requires skill, the skill of being attuned to subtle sensing. How can you know such things? Simple, you are life's expression unfolding in every moment. Trust that.

Ego asks: (endlessly) separating

Is life expanding or contracting?

Is life movement or stillness?

Is life eternal or fleeting?

Is life Yin or Yang?

Life Asks: (endlessly) testing

Can you expand as you contract?

Can you move and breathe in empty stillness?

Can you be fully present in this moment?

Can you *contain* both Yin and Yang?

It is Ego to endlessly argue. Life needs but one answer – Yes!

53.

On Seekers

Throughout my life, I have known so many spiritual seekers. They're my people. We had that in common - Seeking spirit, such a worthy pursuit. We were endlessly, tirelessly talking about it, thinking about it, reading and discussing books about it. Wonderful friendships effortlessly came into being and faded away again through the years. Then a curious thing happened to come to mind. For all the talking, thinking and readings no one was getting any closer to it. How elusive this something called spirit was proving to be.

For all the talk about gaining a new perspective on things, it didn't seem to be having any noticeable effect. John still incessantly complained about his relationship with his wife. Judy still kept going on and on about the annoying people at her higher consciousness seminars. And me, I talked a good game, but still felt the need to pound a few beers just about every weekend. What sweet relief it was to find out that Chogyam Trungpa got hammered as much as I did! Real spiritual growth was nowhere to be seen. Something wasn't right. I knew I was in trouble when my oldest son asked, "Dad, don't you care about enlightenment anymore?" I took a long pull of Fosters and answered, "I'm as enlightened as I ever was." The scary thing about it was, I meant it.

I knew what I was doing. I was enjoying my life. I liked drinking beer. It's not like I was unconscious... Yeah, right.

It's not what you say, it's what you do. What I was doing, what all my fellow seekers were doing was talking ourselves out of doing anything that would change things. "I'm OK, you're OK, let me get this one." I could come up with a dozen good reasons why it didn't matter. If I talked long enough, maybe the feeling that I wasn't in touch with the real sources of my discontent would be spiritually transformed, or transmuted, or just go the hell away. It didn't work - So, now what? Hard training, that's what. I needed a new set of rules that didn't give me so much wiggle room. I settled on two.

Rule #1: Stay sober. Rule #2: Do whatever it takes not to break Rule #1. To be honest, the whole 12 step thing seemed to be a bit excessive. Though I must admit that giving myself over to a higher power was the key upon which it all rested. Was there back sliding? Yes, but that didn't change the rules. Finally, I made a vow and held it close. It was hard, but it worked.

Bottom line – If spiritual growth is what you want, you've got to get serious. Half-hearted efforts and paying it lip-service just won't do. You've got to know that your ego is going to go: "Enlightenment? You bet! Let's do it. It's you and me all the way to Nirvana!" But if you're serious you'll realize that it's a trip only the "you" part can make. The "me" stuff has to be seen for what it is. The "me" stuff is the problem.

Sometimes I miss beer-drinking Bill. We were friends for a long time. Friends, hell - I loved the guy. But like being born and dying, the path to spirit has to be walked naked and alone. It's just the way it is.

54.

Dreaming The Ego's Dream

Have you ever been in the middle of a conversation with someone and somewhere along the line you have the distinct feeling that they are no longer listening to you, then moments later they are? Then they're not, and so on? You feel that way because that's what's really going on! They can't help it. Their thought stream, perhaps prompted by what you are saying, takes off in a different direction and pulls their attention from you to them. It's always about them isn't it?

It's natural to be offended. After all, you have something to say. That is, until you notice they're not listening. Then you try to recapture their attention by saying something about them, knowing full well that *that* will get their attention. Then you let them say something so it can be about them again for a few minutes before you steer it all to being about you again. We call this strange little dance – communication.

At the beginning of every human friendship there is that wonderful phase of things where we really want to plumb the depths of another's experiences. We're riveted by the other's story. There is an evolutionary imperative that tells us – pay attention! This is important! We perk up whenever we sense a golden opportunity to gain the knowledge imparted by experience without having to go through the experience ourselves. It's what we humans do. It's why we talk. Most of the time however, it is only beneficial to the degree that we find what the other has to say compatible with our habitual stream of thought. Sometimes, somehow we "click." It fits. We're on the same page. Don't you love it? But what is it clicking with? What is it fitting into? It is our picture or concept of 'me' - The construction that we've made of our particular point of view to give it substance – Ego. You're not really experiencing another person, your projecting all you love about yourself onto them. Just like Narcissus, the Ego is fascinated gazing in to the 'pool' of another and seeing its own reflection – for a while. This is the 'honeymoon' phase of the relationship; then all too soon, the old "Hey! What about me?" ego-mind returns and the honeymoon's over. As ego-mind resumes control, that fascinating "sameness" starts to dissolve into "differences". Why? Because that's the fundamental organizing principle at work in the ego - mind: differentiate, separate, negate. That mind, for the most part, creates a case for what something is not, yet the impression is perceived as if it is affirming what is. What a dirty trick! Is it any wonder that the majority of your thinking is so negative? Ego-mind is always pulling everything apart. Divide and conquer is its essential strategy, and right there is where real relationships begin to dissolve from our sight.

Everything connected to everything else is the truth of creation. Everything separate from everything else is the ruthlessly enforced criteria of ego-mind. In the light of truth, it is revealed for what it is – a fictitious entity held together solely by its own relentless insistence of being separate from everything else. Without that inviolable stance, it simply ceases to exist. It can't be blamed for that. It wants to live, just like you and I. Once discovered, we needn't declare war on it. After all, it is a part of our own dear self. Yet, as Abraham Lincoln so wisely intoned, "A house divided against itself cannot stand." We simply can't allow it to continue its rule. It is a parasite, a virus. A bug in the program. What is more, it is the source of our fall from grace; the grace of seeing 'what is' clearly. A compassionate response is what is required towards diminishing the ego's insistent view. Be as gentle with yourself as you would be with an innocent, fearful child awakening from a nightmare. The ego is simply dreaming an ego's dream. That is all that it can do. Knowing it isn't real and never was, is all that is required.

55.

A Day on the Hill

When I was 59 years old I took my 16 month old grandson sledding for the first time. I had a ball. I'd launched myself enthusiastically down the hill a half a dozen times before I became aware that all the other adults were just hanging out at the top. They seemed to be enjoying themselves, but nobody was sledding. Nobody but the kids that is – and me. I had so much fun belly-flopping after my little guy on Saturday, we went again on Sunday.

During short conversations with some of the other gray-haired ones while waiting for the hill to clear, I discovered they were all younger than I was. Yet, all but one declined the offer of borrowing my Sno-Tube for a run, even after I shared how wonderfully it cushioned the ride. The one sporting fellow who took me up on my offer had such difficulty getting on (and off at the bottom) that I felt a little guilty about being the one responsible for putting him through it all. He wasn't very flexible. The guilt quickly dissipated however when he returned to the top of the hill with a huge grin on his face, but "Once was enough!" was his reply at further offers. The whole experience was wonderfully revealing.

These silly practices have imparted their gifts so subtly that I hardly notice anymore. Tai Chi Chih and Harmony Qigong aren't particularly aerobic. Most days I don't even break a sweat. While sledding however, I caught my breath faster than my 14 year old son after climbing the hill, and I was the one carrying my grandson! I overheard someone at the top sagely declaring, "He'll pay for it tomorrow." That never happened. There was no price other than the delightful "return to childhood" the whole experience proved to be. My time on that hill was so simple – so profound, so counter to what all of the other "mature adults" were experiencing. The naturally occurring flexibility of body and mind, the fruit of daily practice of breathing, moving, relaxing, was innocently, joyously, effortlessly evident. What great fun!

Life is supposed to be fun....

You know that, right?

56.

Know Thyself

You are a creation of the universe. You are made of star-stuff. The intelligence, physical laws and influences of the cosmos are manifest in you. The edict, "Know Thyself" inscribed on the Temple of Apollo at Delphi is a bit of timeless wisdom that deserves our attention. Our focused attention is what is required to accomplish it.

Every human being that I have known intimately has brought a precious gift into my life, the insight into the world of another's experience. Intimacy comes from being compassionately open to those experiences without internal judgment, criticism or agreement; in simply allowing their voice to be heard. Be still and listen. You must be present for a meaningful exchange to occur. Intimate relationship is part and parcel of the human experience. Perhaps not as essential for survival as food, clothing, and shelter, but definitely on the same playing field as social interaction and sex.

However, even though there is this fundamental push toward intimacy inherent in every human heart, recognized or not, we seldom seek to satisfy it in the most useful way imaginable – becoming intimate with your self.

This is the purpose of every mystery school or secret society that has ever existed. It lies at the heart of healing, the return to wholeness - Know Thyself.

In getting to know anyone intimately we have to spend some time with them. Watching, listening, tuning in with our subtle senses to get a 'feel' of where they're coming from. The same things are required in getting to know yourself. That relationship is the most important relationship of your life.

You and your self, sounds strange doesn't it? As if there were two of you. I've got news for you. There are a whole lot more than two! One of the chief impediments to true communication is this - even if you know someone intimately, you can never know which of their many selves you're talking to!

For instance, let's say you offer a bit of well-meaning constructive criticism to your spouse or significant other – innocent enough, "Have you ever tried it this way?" You could get - "I'm not stupid!" as a response if the self-doubter is awake and rumbling around inside of them. You could get their "I'm loved and cared for" self and get a smile and "Wow, I would have never thought of that. Thanks!" Even an emotionally volatile explosion of things suddenly flying through the air as they storm outraged from the room is a very real possibility you'd never see coming. I've received each and every one of those responses from a wonderful human being that I loved wth all my heart.

Eckhart Tolle calls that sleeping dragon within us all, the pain body. It's an accumulation of all the pain you've inherited as a member of the human race as well as a conglomeration of all the hurts you've personally experienced. It may be active or asleep. When roused, all it wants, all it knows, is pain. Its sole agenda is to create more pain to feed on. It revels in it. Pain is all it knows because pain is what it is. Like attracts like - it's the law.

When awakened from its slumber it reeks havoc on all it surveys until like a satiated beast, it goes back to sleep. That is, until it's once again roused by a trigger, usually the same words or situation that created it. Then it reappears with all the fury, or resentment, or cruelty, or depression and self-loathing that created it in the first place; leaving lives and relationships in shambles. This is the destructive propensity we must all overcome. It is a hero's quest; a battle that must be waged, requiring a special kind of courage. This dark shadow is the relentless enemy of your peace and well-being. It is the destroyer of love, because love is its un-doing. In the light of love the dark shadow is shown for what it is, a phantom of the past, a ghost of pain unhealed. And in that blazing light of awareness it withers and dies

Eckhart suggests watching for its awakening and immediately shining the light of our awareness upon it. A skill I feel is powerfully developed in regular Qigong practice. This is perhaps Qigong's greatest gift, creating an inner condition of subtle body awareness that makes it possible to see what is arising within.

You are the producer, director and star of the movie you call your life. It's a *great* movie! You're going to get sucked in, no doubt about it. What a story! Life, death, love, hate, triumph, disaster, every emotion possible, and Ooooh - touching, tasting, and let's not forget sex! The idea is not to be so spiritual that you transcend it. (Sorry it can't be done, I don't care what anybody says.) The idea is to be it, all of it. "The whole catastrophe" as Zorba the Greek would say. There is nothing that you are not. Accept that. Revel in it. I think it is the way we are made in God's image – There is nothing that we are not. That is the magic. That is the mystery.

57.

On Fitness

Qigong is nothing less than the most efficient energy management system ever devised. It is an extremely effective exercise program as well. It is a different approach to the age old axiom of "First - Do no harm."

How many people do you know that have never hurt themselves exercising? That have never awakened sore from the "beneficial" exertions of the day before. How about you? The "no pain, no gain" approach to greater health is, it seems to me, a bit of an oxymoron. There's a better way of keeping the old engine "tip top" than taking it up to 100 plus to "blow the carbon out". If you're going to "throw a rod" that'll be when it happens – believe me.

Life is soft and pliable. It has to be to change and grow, which in case you haven't noticed is what life is always and endlessly doing. How to stay soft and pliable is the challenge. Rock hard abs are *not* helping anything. Yet at this point in time they seem to be the symbol of fitness in the West. What's that all about? Do you have rock hard abs? Does anyone you know have rock hard abs?

There are quite a few runners in my neighborhood. I see them all the time and they're *never* smiling. Their facial expressions are those of a person who's been shot, or at least in a lot of pain. I live in the Southwest suburbs of Chicago. Every year someone in my experience is training to run in the Chicago Marathon. Every year thousands of my fellow Midwesterners run 26 miles for the hell of it. It sounds like hell to me. Doesn't anyone remember that the messenger who ran all the way to Athens from the plains of marathon, delivered his message, and then promptly died? I always tease my students that if they ever see me running around town, to take out the guy running behind me, because he's trying to catch and kill me. That's when I'll run. Under those circumstances it would be the natural thing to do, otherwise I'm walking.

Practice your Qigong. If you need to run, you'll be able to run – if you have to. You'll be able to climb, belly crawl, or any thing else you have to do. Qigong will keep you fit. It will keep you strong, in a very meaningful and useful way.

Learning to conserve your energy is a wiser, better way of guaranteeing you'll have it when you need it. Work, but do it in a relaxed way. Move with skill and precision. Breathe openly and efficiently. Be aware of what you're doing as much as possible and accidents will not find you. When it comes to pain I'm with Daffy Duck who cracked me up when he sagely declared, "I don't like pain – it hurts me."

58.

The Heart Has its Reasons

The movement or influence of spirit seems to the thinking mind – illogical. Take a spiritual tradition in one culture and introduce it to another and the result is often wildly unpredictable. For instance, for thousands of years the Eastern spiritual tradition did little to transform the society in which it arose. In a sense, it was but a side-bar, learned by rote and generally acknowledged, but had almost completely lost its power to act as a catalyst for real change. This is the inevitable downside of "tradition" as it succumbs to the natural cycle of decaying into thoughtless action.

Take that same perennial wisdom, expose a different culture to it (one to which it is foreign) and that transformative power is miraculously unleashed from the fetters of complacency in which it was held. When it is "new" again, its original power is born again. The perennial theme of resurrection and renewal holds sway once more, and the society in which that occurs experiences not only the dynamic influx of the spiritual energy from which such wisdom originally emerged, but the energy of that knowing is transmuted in the process and arises even more powerfully as a hybrid of what it once was, and what it has now become.

Whatever powers that be will inevitably be undermined and accelerated toward dissolution as a result. Because the ego-mind never saw it coming, (how could it?) the mental resistance to such change will at least equal the power of the 'new' trying to emerge. How it all plays out is ultimately determined by its acceptance or rejection in each human heart. It has been said, "The heart has its reasons that reason knows nothing of." The heart recognizes what the mind cannot. The human heart is the organ of perception of the spiritual realm. It is through the human heart that spirit finds its way most powerfully into the world.

59.

This Is Relating?

This is the clearest explanation of the most common mode of human interaction I've ever read:

> *You have a mental image not only of who the other person is, but also of who you are, especially in relation to the person you are interacting with. So you are not relating with that person at all, but who you think the other person is and vice versa. The conceptual image your mind has made of yourself is relating to its own creation which is the conceptual image it has made of the other person. The other person's mind has probably done the same, so every egoic interaction between two people is in reality the interaction between four conceptual mind-made realities that are ultimately fictions. It is therefore not surprising there is so much conflict in relationships. There is no true relationship.*

~ Eckhart Tolle, *A New Earth*, p.94

Does that sound right to you? Does it have to be so? Not at all, not once you recognize what is happening. This is why you should *never* beat yourself up for being unconscious. It is only through becoming deeply aware, that you will ever *realize* you are being unconscious – *and then you're not* – POOF! Just like that. It's over.

Sure, it's tough when you're feeling like the brunt of a great cosmic joke. And yet, once you get it - that it's all you, and always has been - it's really quite funny! How clever you are. Have a good laugh. It's good for you!

60.

Save The Earth?

Today is one of those gray days. It's misting, not raining, cool not cold. It's a perfect Midwestern first week of March day. Most days are perfect when I'm clear that it's not about me, it's not about us. It's about the Earth. We don't need to save the Earth. The Earth will be fine. It has survived meteors and comets crashing into it hundreds of times, at hundreds of thousands of miles and hour. It will survive humanity. That's also true of life on earth. Life will always find a way. Where the whole "save the planet" thing breaks down is with us.

If we're honest about it, it's not about saving the planet at all. It's about saving ourselves. If we do not change our ways *we* won't be here. We'll be gone. The earth isn't going anywhere. We are. 99.9% of all species that ever lived are gone. I'd say it's fairly obvious that whenever we contemplate where mankind will be in another 10,000 years we should definitely allow for the 99.9% chance that we will be gone too. The fact that we don't is part of the problem. It's almost as if we are incapable of imagining a universe without us. We take so much for granted. A world without us? Impossible!

I'm not a doomsdayer or a doomsayer, but there isn't a day that goes by that I don't take a moment and see myself dead. I think it's a very reasonable and healthy thing to do. A world without Bill Nielsen is an inevitable, inexorable reality. I think we should all entertain the notion a lot more often that we do.

Why? Does it change the way I act? The way I relate to people? Does it change the world at all? Yes, yes and yes.

You and I are influencing the ultimate form and function of human life on planet Earth. Consciously or not, we are constantly subtly transforming the life energy flowing through us. In so doing we are also transforming the lives of others as well. How they see the world is influenced by how you see it. It is a shared vision. So, how do you see it? Are you fighting your way through it as if it is a never ending war? Does life's unpredictability scare you or energize you? Can you learn to embrace it all, loving it for all it's worth? Despite what you may think, seeing the world without you; seeing a world with all of humanity dead and gone isn't sick at all. It isn't morbid. In fact, it serves to shine a loving light on the precious role we play. Like Jimmy Stewart in *It's a Wonderful Life*, you have no idea how different the world would be without you.

Try this. Try this right now. Take a moment to relax, take a few breaths, in 2-3-4- out 2-3-4 – breathe and feel – then ask yourself: "In this moment where do I stand in relation to life?" There is no right or wrong answer. What you feel in your heart answers the question. That's where you begin.

Try it.

I'm serious.

Try it right now.

61.

In Search of Truth

I find it curious that so many of my students are hesitant to embrace any notion that runs afoul of their religious beliefs. I was raised Roman Catholic until I was eight or so and then spent a few years being bussed to Billy Graham crusades during my evangelical experience as a teenaged Southern Baptist. Needless to say, the Christian orientation of the world is something that comes quite naturally to me.

The main problem that I have with that orientation is how much the espoused Christian tradition differs from what the man, Jesus the Christ, actually said. I know I'm opening up a can of worms here. The realization that all the words written may not be accurate after all the time, translations, and interpretations they've gone through, lies at the forefront of my thinking about such matters.

That aside, I love books in general. I have probably read a couple of thousand by now and the thought that any one of them would (or could) exclusively claim to be the Truth, let alone, the word of God seems quite absurd. A book is a book, nothing more, nothing less.

Books to me are such beautiful things. For years I couldn't bear the thought of writing in one. I find them somehow sacred compilations of the thoughts of men and women, some long dead; evidence of where we've come from, speculations on where we're headed. They are the written records of all the "Truths" that have ruled men's lives across the millennia; tomes of the times in which they lived. The ever-changing views of the "reality" expressed in each of them that have somehow shaped our world never cease to fascinate and amaze me. Yet, in the end it is only a world of thought, constructions of the mind, an edifice of ideas. Is it reality or sheer imagination? Who can say? In the world of men, one civilization after another, arose and fell on the fickle shifting sands of popular opinion. Is there really such a thing as progress?

How seriously we take it all, once we agree to do so. As if all of eternity rests upon our interpretation, our embrace or denial of "what is." What is, so fleeting, so unstable, there really is no – "the way things are." Bodies of star stuff, empires of culture, Gods of every description, appearing and disappearing as they each contribute their moment of being to some vast ineffable purpose. That is reality.

It's kind of scary when you think about it. And that's the point. I'm convinced that we come up with all this stuff just to support this inner structure of 'me' or 'us' so we can remain in our comfortably deluded reality. Give it all a story, then let the story prove it true. "I don't know" is not an option. That's not truth, that's mass delusion. "You can't handle the truth!" Jack Nicholson bellows in one of his most memorable scenes. How true…. How true.

You are here. Life goes on. It is what it is - True, true and true. Read the last few sentences again. Feel the words. That's it in a nutshell isn't it?

It's us or them. Only the strong survive. God's on our side. God wants us to _____ (your choice, fill in the blank.) Can you feel the difference?

You know the truth in your heart, but your mind can't grasp it. Mind is relative- Truth absolute.

Mind is ☯   Truth is ◯

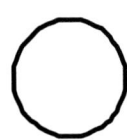

Truth is the background upon which, within which the Yin and Yang of creation appears. It is the space in which all things manifest and become. It is into that same emptiness all manifestation eventually dissolves. It has always been. It will always be. It is eternal. It is where we come from. It is what we'll return to. It is ultimately what we are.

IS-ness

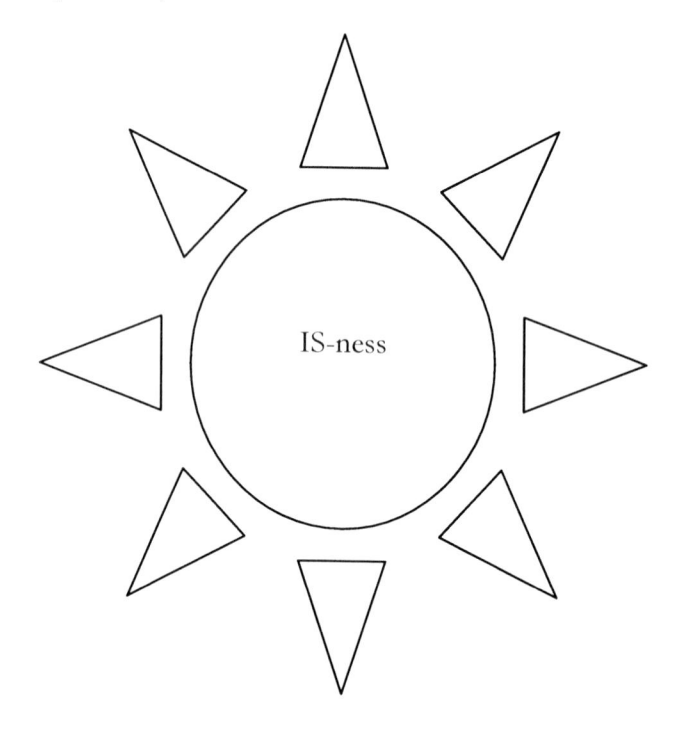

And that's the Truth!

62.

The Enigma of Knowing Nothing

I've been meditating on and off for decades. Transcendental meditation was my very first practice. It changed my life. It taught me to be still. It taught me that I could be aware of nothing – no thing and still be awake. I learned much, though most of what I learned I can't tell you about. There are no words because words are designed to express something, not nothing. You can see the problem.

These days, Nothing keeps popping up. Thoughts just stop, and there is only this shining. It's there, just under the covers, when I'm thinking. It's *really* there when I'm not. Eyes open or closed, it's there. Whether I'm alone or having a conversation, it's there. It's the most natural thing in the world. (That sentence sounds silly.) How about - It is that upon which the world appears. It is that from which all arises. It is nothing, and yet feels pregnant and full. It is the space in which every "thing" exists. It is the silence from which sound arises. It is the spaces between the words.

I used to meditate to hopefully find it in the midst of all the mental noise. I craved a respite from confusion and chaos. I wanted to escape, to be free of the din, like the scene in a war movie where the bomb goes off, and everything goes suddenly quiet, and our hapless hero is experiencing images only.

All at once, a connection has been broken and the processing just stops, there are images, but no interpretation. What's happening? Who can say? It's just images on a screen. Stuff piled on stuff. "Why add stuff to Self?" Steven would say.

Now, thoughts are like clouds drifting by, mind like the sound of electricity, humming as it moves through the wires. The world feels like a movie and there's this great big huge nothing shining through all of it. It's as if while watching the clouds, all of a sudden there's an opening and this huge shining overwhelms my sight. The clouds disappear from my awareness, and there is only blinding brilliance. Other times it's more subtle, like something rustling in the leaves in the quiet of deep woods. Then a breeze arises (as the mind moves) and all the leaves start moving with it. Yet, I know it's not gone, just obscured.

Qigong dissolves the clouds. It stills the wind. It allows the seeing and hearing of nothing to occur. It teaches you about stillness, movement, breath, life; the whole enchilada, all without even closing your eyes.

It feels like sitting and meditating isn't really necessary. It also feels like meditating brought me here. How strange that it should feel like an indulgence. So often in meditation, when the world disappears, what I can only call the *truth* appears in its place. Without even trying, the 'you' you've always known dissolves and you *are* the truth. You are the seeing itself manifested as that reflection you see when you look in the mirror. That's not really you. Your eyes are designed to see whatever light bounces off of. It is the light behind them that truly sees. It is you who are shining the world into existence. Without that you in the mirror, there is only nothing, longing to become.

It all begins and ends there.

63.

The Dragon's Path.

"You'll never get rich teaching Qigong" my father said. "Most people want things done for them. They don't want to have to do it for themselves." The last 10 years of my father's life were pretty miserable. Likewise, his view of it became pretty miserable as well. He died at 72, a very sick man. Everything that was wrong with him compounding his ill health until it was all too much. He had migraine headaches almost every month of his life. High blood pressure, two heart attacks, adult onset diabetes, kidney failure, he was a mess. Yet he never did anything to heal himself, but quit smoking. He walked his talk, I'll give him that. He was always one helluva teacher. He was perfect. He taught me again and again, just by being who he was, what not to be. It was he more than anyone else who set my feet upon the Dragon's Path.

What is the Dragon's Path? The Dragon's Path is when the path that you are walking appears beneath your feet with every step you take. If you were to turn and look behind you, there would be no sign to indicate where you've been. As you look ahead, there is no path to follow; to lead you on your way. It is there beneath each footfall – and then it's gone. It holds no promise. It asks no price. It is what is.

When I was younger it grieved me deeply that I had no footsteps in which to follow. No loving hand to guide me. As I grew older, I realized I also stood in no one's shadow. I was always free to find my own way. Once I understood the Dragon's Path, I saw it for what it was; the way of life itself.

64.

The Circle of Life

If you ever watched *The Lion King* you're probably very familiar with "The Circle of Life" theme. Yet, you may not know that it looks like this:

The great circle-ation (often spelled circulation) is nothing less than the "way" of Life. There are stars orbiting galaxies; planets orbiting stars; moons orbiting planets, planets turning on center, turbines turning generators, crankshafts turning driveshafts, and on and on and on…

The circulation of energy turning into everything and then back to energy again is happening everywhere in everyway, at all times, through all dimensions, forever.

Now you see it   now you don't. Poof! ………….. Magic!

If you've never seen *The Lion King*, I highly recommend it. It's a modern rendition of the perennial wisdom of how the vicissitudes of life can cause an unconscious disconnection from our own inner Knowing; how easily joy turns to misery, and the process of discovering and dispelling our inner demons. It touches upon our innocence, our natural inheritance, the loss of the realization of who and what we are, through guilt and fear; the regaining of out true power through aligning our masculine and feminine energies, it's all there. The journey of life is there, artfully and skillfully expressed with imagination and humor. *The Lion King* is *not* a kid's movie. Watch it with an open heart and you'll be amazed at what you'll see, and the soundtrack isn't bad either!

65.

Mind

The mind is constantly making promises it can't keep. If a friend of yours pulled the kind of crap on you your mind does, you would not consider them a friend. It tells you only what you want to hear. It will never say, "the emperor has no clothes." Ignorance is called that because we are ignoring what is. We are looking for answers where they cannot, will not, *ever* be found. We're like the mystic fool mullah Nasrudin in Sufi teaching stories, looking for his keys under the lamppost. "Where did you lose them?" his friend inquires. "In my house," says the mullah. "Why are you looking out here then?" he asks. "There's more light out here," the mullah replies.

    The mind is like a bird pecking at thoughts. "Is this something? – Is this something?" When it compares what was once to what is, it tells you that what *is* is what was, and you believe it! The problem being that what is simply is. It never was before, it won't be again, and yet the mind says, "Oh! I know this." It doesn't know anything! It just refers everything to everything else 'til it comes up with a match and puts a label on it for reference and files it and that makes it another "something" it can refer to later. The mind is a slight of hand artist. It's the purveyor of a shell game without a pea. It deals in phantoms only, because the mind itself is a phantom. It's only a process. It organizes. It makes patterns and then stores and refers to those patterns. It doesn't "know" anything. If you are identified with it, if you "think" you are your mind, you can't see that you are referring only to a process and calling it "me". You are the mechanism in which, through which, the process occurs. In that sense, "I think therefore I am," is 100% undiluted bullshit.

66.

A Little One on One with Source

Here in the West the spiritual aspect of our lives is rarely even acknowledged in our day to day existence. One could easily understand how Muslims who are called to prayer five times a day would view a Christian society called to prayer for an hour on Sunday mornings, essentially Godless. And essentially godless we are. The average American (65% in the latest poll) states a belief in a supreme being. We just don't act like we believe in a supreme being. We're way too busy with more important things like going to work and making money and getting things done. Even our connection with our church of faith is more often an act of conscience or habit than a way of life. We don't get involved with much one-on-one with Source.

"Hey, wait a minute!" you say. "It's not like that at all." Really… be honest. When's the last time you sat still for a time in silence? When's the last time you actually felt the peace or presence of God? When's the last time you were still enough to actually feel the life vibrating within you? When was the last time you felt a deep and abiding gratitude for the miracle of your existence – even in a church?

Please don't feel like I'm judging. I'm not. It is how it is. Our society does not support spirit. On the list of important things to do today, being still and acknowledging the spirit within you is probably way down on the list; just after "scoop out the cat box."

The great thing about Qigong is you do it as "Get some exercise" or "Take a break." If you put that on the list, preferably somewhere near the top, the presence, the vibration, the gratitude will spontaneously arise as a result. You become one of the wise few instead of the foolish many. You effortlessly accomplish the most important thing you have to do today, to experience and acknowledge your true nature; to transcend what society and family and even you assign importance to, and attend to what is truly important in the greater scheme of things. Embracing and acknowledging the beauty and mystery of life itself. You relax, you breathe, you feel - Holy, Holy, Sanctus, Sanctus.

67.

On Climbing

Why would anyone want to be enlightened anyway? What's the point? "I like my life. I enjoy my job. I feel blessed, and I'm pretty happy with things as they are," you say. Good for you. You *are* blessed. Chances are you are also physically healthy, mentally and emotionally balanced, and deeply connected to your spiritual center. You are in your natural state. You are poised, centered, and aware. How wonderful.

Yet, there is the distinct possibility that the delicate balance underpinning your present condition will inevitably be assailed by ill health, mental stress, and emotional trauma. The world will continue to pull and tug at you. Trials are coming your way. It's not if, but when. That's the reality. A balanced life is a delicate thing.

What we need is a little insurance, not the kind you buy, the kind you cultivate. The influences that knock us for a loop are rarely the tsunami kind (although there will be times…) they are more the little waves licking at the shore; day in, day out. What seems so firm and supportive now, is slowly eroding away, and you may suddenly find yourself on less than solid ground. Don't let the world erode your foundation. Spend a little time each day contributing to your own stability. It's not so much where you stand that will determine life's outcomes, as how you stand in relation to life that makes the difference.

When I was a child I discovered a wonderful old giant white pine tree ideal for climbing. It was huge. The branches were sturdy and well spaced and each time I visited that old tree, I'd climb a little higher than the time before, the promise of a broader vista egging me on. In time I was climbing to a height just a few feet from the very top. The view was incredible. I could see for miles, and began to enjoy the gentle swaying of the treetop in the wind that sent little shots of adrenaline coursing through me. I was thrilled and terrified all at once. What a feeling! I loved it!! I could never quite resist the impulse to go and climb that tree a few times every summer. Then, for whatever reason, my usual perch gave way beneath me (I was growing after all) and though I only fell a few feet, tree climbing suddenly lost its allure. From then on, the fear outweighed the thrill and I quit climbing. I was being prudent - wise. Yet something was lost.

Life's like that isn't it? There is a narrowing of the way. Self imposed limitations find their way into our experience. More often than not it's got something to do with fear, the 'Don't go there' signs popping up within. It's how we're made. On the one hand it's about survival, we're being prudent. On the other, we miss our tree, our lofty view...it needn't be so.

There are other ways of attaining a broader view, of challenging our self- imposed limitations. We need to relax. To feel our fear, anxieties, and worries and not feed them is a skill that must be practiced. Like tree climbing, we need only go as far as we can go and then rest there for a while. In cultivating our willingness to engage with our apprehensions we rob them of their power, instead of the other way around. Fear is simply saying "Be very aware." It's nothing to be afraid of. Instead of climbing a swaying tree, it becomes more like climbing a pyramid. Ever higher still being the possibility, but without being exposed to the danger of the instability of the structure that supports you.

The practice of Qigong is building that pyramid, a foundation of support with every deep, relaxing breath. It seems so fragile and yet when you feel the fear and do it anyway, that on which you stand the earthquakes in life cannot topple, cannot sway; that life's tsunamis, however huge, cannot wash away. And Oh my goodness....what a view! That's the icing on the cake.

68.

The Occasional Apocalypse

Every once in a while this creative process we call life takes a wrong turn and heads down a blind alley. This energy in motion some call God is never supposed to make a mistake. In reality it never does. However when you're dealing with everything that is and have eternity to work with, you've go to admit, it allows for a bit of flexibility. Let's just focus for a moment on this little relationship of "God and Man'. In all of creation there are all kinds (and levels) of interactive energies playing out countless scenarios.

Galactic energy – Star machines, are in plentiful supply. Even more so, the star energies themselves create the stuff of worlds: light, gravity, electromagnetism, complex elements and most importantly life.

Life energies are more subtle and quite fragile. Yet they effortlessly create the perfect vehicle for consciousness to be expressed in very diverse ways. Though I fundamentally agree (and I am deeply disturbed by having to refer to myself as a fundamentalist) that consciousness is all there is, it seems that man possesses more of it, in the smallest package, than anything yet discovered. So it would seem to me that humankind fills a rather unique niche in this moving energy matrix.

Without building a cumbersome philosophical structure I'm just going to ask you to take that on faith. (oh no, I *am* a fundamentalist!)

The concept that we serve creation through being a harvest of consciousness energy is not new. However, I don't think of it as having quite the good versus evil tone that generally accompanies that view. Let's just use a good ol' farming analogy here.

Creation found a certain efficiency in having so much consciousness energy available for recycling in the human condition. It keeps our nurturing environment just stable enough to keep us growing and alive so it has sufficient consciousness energy to keep growing and refining its own creative processes.

However consciousness energy is a fickle thing. There is no guarantee that as a single seed comes to fruition it will produce enough to nourish and expand its processes. If a human being (or more accurately, a human animal) doesn't meet the requirement of expanding its consciousness energy, in accord with its design, more individuals will be needed to fulfill the required "consciousness energy" requirements of the process that initiated it. Creation's purposes (and requirements) come first. No other agenda will be considered paramount. It is what it is. So however humbling it may be, we are first and foremost grist for the mill.

Whatever values we ascribe to our proliferation and survival mean nothing in the greater scheme. As the "consciousness energy" within humankind diminishes through lack of the expansion of consciousness called for in the original design, more of us would be required to serve (or sacrifice) the energetic requirements for which we were destined.

Desperate times call for desperate measures. Greater consciousness will be served regardless. First, the universe creates more of us. A natural response to its need. When even that fails to supply the required consciousness quota, the stability of our nurturing environment becomes unstable and there's a huge 'filling of the coffers of creation' as consciousness energy is released enmass from the level of the physical. What is lacking in quality is made up in quantity. It's not personal; it's just inherent in the design. Life feeds life.

If we play our roles efficiently and well, balance reigns and the subtler realms of existence integrate and expand ad infinitum. If we fail to integrate and expand our consciousness energy to a sufficient degree, we simply become one more wrong turn, one more blind alley and life goes on – without us.

99.9% of all species ever created through this process no longer exist. The odds are not in our favor. However, there is a *huge* potential in humanity for a concentration of consciousness energy to be extremely efficient in contributing to all of Life's purposes, and in so doing, insure the continuation of our own. The problem is, we have to choose to cooperate with those purposes. We have to embody greater and greater conscious awareness. Then we are no longer a problem. We are a solution. Ever-expanding consciousness sufficiently developed and integrated whether it is local (ours) or non-local (universal) is priority one. The modus operandi of humanity and that of creation itself are one and the same. We don't have to die to offer it up. When we simply live up to our potential there's more than enough to go around, once you and I awaken to the reality that that's what we're here to do. From then on a new level of conscious human interaction with creation becomes a real possibility. Most importantly, in serving Life's purposes we automatically chart a course that best insures our own survival as a species. Yet I must admit, I have the distinct feeling that we're running out of time.

69.

High School Days

I hated high school. I was always getting kicked out for stupid reasons. I got sent home once for not having a belt on my jeans. Another time I was told to go home and shave. I had never shaved. Not yet. Needless to say, after having to walk the seven miles home (and then deal with my crazy father) I grew a bit apathetic about rules and schools. My attitude was reflected in my grades. The teachers responsible for my trips to the office were appropriately compensated for their transgressions. They got a lot of attitude and I got a lot of F's. It was often stated that I was "uncooperative" and "not living up to my potential". Hey, they started it! Besides, James Dean was my hero in those days. So I'd ask myself, what would he do? That's what I did

I wasn't all attitude though, there were a couple of teachers that were really passionate about what they taught. The ones I liked best would teach for days without cracking the book. I loved that about them. The A's and B's I got in their classes told the story. To this day, I love geography and physical science and strangely enough, business law. (I flunked out of French and ended up there). I had passion, they had passion, theirs was focused mine was not. So while I was in their class their passion became my passion.

To this day I can't resist putting names to the shapes of states or countries on a map in a news magazine. Quantum physics and the latest scientific discoveries continue to fascinate me, and the latest daily dealings on Wall Street have me crying out for at least an appearance of corporate accountability (not to mention a bit more humanity in the dealings of the business world).

I could say "That's just the way I am" and that would be partly true. To say that those passionate few in high school weighted things in a certain direction would be a more accurate assessment of how

I came to be the way I am. Without their influence where or how would I be? Who can say?

Whenever the thought "That's how I am" appears – STOP! Look to the happenstance, coincidence and pure chance that played a role in creating this fictional 'I' that's any way at all. Passions, likes, dislikes, judgments, all this stuff piled into a heap is certainly there, it's just no 'I'. It's just stuff. Past experiences filed under "DANGER – EMOTIONALLY CHARGED." Whenever you experience a trigger: a situation, a word, a certain look – BAM! – you react as if it is happening again! The truth is, whatever is happening never happened before. You are responding to a memory only. You have to become conscious enough to catch that. You have to have a small, still, space between the world of experience and your knee-jerk reaction in order to see what's really happening NOW.

Have you ever found yourself thinking "I need some space?" You're absolutely right. You do, but it's up to you to create it, and it takes practice, lots of practice. You are in essence, reprogramming the machine. It's a challenge alright but it can be done, one realization at a time. Every time you truly "see" what's happening you're not reacting, you're not unconscious anymore, and that is a very, *very* good thing. Within that small space of clear seeing in that tiny moment of presence, divorced from the past, peace resides, and joy finds fertile soil in which to grow.

70.

It's All About Patterns

I don't really know whether or not it's true that the average person only uses 10% of their brain's potential capacity. I think it might be an urban legend, a myth. On the other hand, it may be that it's an indication of that sneaking suspicion we all have about not living up to our potential. (See, your mother was right!) We all know we could be using our brainpower a little more effectively, but how do we pull it off?

If we all know it's possible, why aren't we doing it? Well, for one thing it's not so much about brain as it is about mind. We equate our intelligence, our ability to think, with our brains. You and I can't help but think. Our brain wants to make patterns. Our awareness responds to those patterns. The first order of business is always to get newer patterns to fit with old ones; to accept or reject newer patterns based on whether or not they fit easily with those already established. My particular pattern pile is called "Bill". Bill is pretty limited by this state of affairs. Could it be that as much as 90% of the stimuli Bill is exposed to resists interaction with previously established patterns? "Whoa! Hold on there! What the hell is *that? That* doesn't fit anywhere – ignore it!" and it hits delete. I suspect the brain is the source of ignore-ance. We're not talking about stupidity here, but ignorance. Stupid is forever. Ignorance can be fixed. How? Here comes the kicker – patterning!

Tai Chi and Qigong take advantage of the brain's bias toward patterning. Creating a pattern is a fundamental part of the practice. The difference is – There is no *identification* with the pattern. This is why it's a good idea to learn a few different styles or forms. It is a very simple way of not getting too attached to a single pattern.

I'm constantly disappointed when I bump into another Qigong practitioner (Lord knows there are few enough of us in these parts) and they are all caught up in who their teacher was and how powerful their particular style is compared to others, blah, blah, blah. I always feel they've somehow missed the point.

One of the things I love about Tai Chi Qigong is, you never master it. It's always just practice. (It would be very beneficial for people to realize that a doctor isn't necessarily a master healer, he's just practicing medicine – on you – remember that). You're practicing patterning. Relax and just watch yourself patterning. After a while you begin very naturally to sustain that particular point of view. Practice regularly, and in time all of the patterns of life are more clearly seen for just what they are, even the "Bill" thing. Energy moving in patterns and forms is what we are designed to see. 100% seeing is what we are. To be firmly grounded in that understanding just takes a bit of patient practice. Trying to find your "self" is like looking for your eyes.

71.

Love Is!

We've all heard that love is what God is. Truer words were never spoken. That is exactly what God is. The question remains, what exactly do you think love is? "Love is patient, love is kind..." Yeah, yeah, I know, I know, and I'm not saying any of that is wrong, it's just too small. Any thought cannot even begin to express it. Love is *huge*. HUGE! It's beyond understanding. It has been said, you cannot speak of the ocean to a well-frog; or of the sky to a songbird in a cage. The mind simply can't grasp the vastness of love. It is that, only the heart of you can know. It is so far beyond the, I love you \ I hate you \ I love you, kind of love. That's not love, that's emotional attachment, a reflection of thought in the body. Love is everything. All of it is one thing. Love is empty, love is blind, love is… STOP! That's it! – Love is.

Inscribe *that* on every church, synagogue, mosque, temple, house and stone. "LOVE IS!" Love is beyond any separation. So it might be a good idea to stop insisting on being a separate "me." "Love hurts," just doesn't ring true. Thinking you're separate from it is what hurts. Love knows no other. Are you in love? Of course you are. How can you not be? Love is playing an eternal game of Hide and Seek with you. Now you see it, now you don't. What love is, ultimately you are. Stop looking for love. You are what you're looking for. It's not out there somewhere. It's right here, right now. At this very moment it is shining out of your eyes and seeing only itself - Everywhere.

72.

The Downside of Belief

Beliefs are only thoughts elevated to a status of reality. We're making something intangible substantial. Don't do it! You'll only suffer. "Belief Thoughts" are what we use to structure not the world, but *our* world. That world is a figment of our collective imagination. What is, is. That's reality. Another word for reality is God.

So what is this "God"? I've heard it's everywhere; in everything; all powerful, all seeing, eternal. So, are we in God? Is God in us? How can it be otherwise? It is only because we believe (think) our thoughts *about* God are real that we say no to what is.

And, we've got all the thoughts we need to back that up! How convenient. "No! I don't believe it! It's not true and I'll tell you why!" Then we artfully show how this or that doesn't fit with certain other thoughts that we have chosen to believe; or should I say, that have remained unquestioned? We artfully create the whole great big package we call our life. It's chock-full of all the why and how thoughts that make it all fit together so nicely and that makes us feel *so* much better, until it clashes with reality and doesn't anymore - all of that effort - for what?

It makes us feel a little less scared. Our little thought cocoon feels safe. So we continue to construct it thought by thought, glue it all together with belief, and call that reality instead. Oh yeah, we're definitely going to suffer.

I already told you about a woman by the name of Byron Katie, and her wonderful book called, *Loving What Is*. After awakening to the reality of what is; she saw so clearly what was creating her suffering – her own unexamined thoughts. She developed a beautifully simple system of self-inquiry she calls "The Work". I highly recommend becoming familiar with it.

It is simple, profound and powerful. It requires only a pencil, paper and a willingness to explore your own unexamined thoughts. You simply ask four questions:

1. Is it true?
2. Can I know absolutely that that is true?
3. How do I react when I have that thought?
4. Who would I be without that thought?

There's a bit more to it, where you turn the thought around, and then you sit with what you've learned for a few minutes. What a beautiful, beautiful, tool she's given us. Thank you Byron Katie!

Are you beginning to see the fundamental error? There is no personal fault in it. It's the way we're made. Some really great new stuff got piled on top of the old stuff. Nature never throws anything away. It simply builds upon all that has worked so far. It's up to you and I to smooth out the rough spots with our intention. Greater awareness in service of greater awareness is our mission, should we decide to accept it. If there's a purpose at all – that's it. And what's the incentive to move in that direction? That's where joy resides. God's love, the universe, reality, call it what you will; in the discovery of Source as what we are, smack dab in the middle of this jumble of 10,000 things, lies the only fulfillment we will ever know. All of this seeking, searching, and longing for that discovery, is the defining attribute of our humanity.

O.K, so we missed the mark. We just lost our way, that's all. Let's forgive ourselves and get on with it. This self-consciousness thing is a relatively new development. There are a few bugs to be worked out. In a world of physical "things" it's a real stretch for an animal to give an invisible nothingness equal attention. Self-consciousness is a real game changer. The tree of knowledge is now in play.

Paying attention to invisible thoughts is a step in the right direction. Paying attention to that from which thoughts arise requires even greater awareness. Yet it is in that crucible of invisible nothingness, of consciousness itself, that the "Elixir of Life" that wonder of wonders that has been sought throughout human history is to be found. I know it.

73.

It's Not Personal

I feel so blessed to have so many wonderful people in my life. As a group I refer to them as my students. In reality they are beautiful emanations of God, Love, Reality – pick one; each and every one of them, my teachers, wise and perfect.

"You'd make a wonderful teacher," my Tai Chi Chih instructor Jeanne Carlson encouraged, all those years ago. I remember at the time I didn't think I was a wonderful anything. I was broke, crippled, separated from my wife, estranged from my best friend, and feeling guilty as hell about all of it. I took everything so personally back then. I didn't know that I was life itself, and I wanted it *my* way. I wanted it to be the way I thought it should be. The thought of changing my mind about how it should be was still a few more months of pain away. I hadn't yet recognized what suffering was for. You can't see clearly when you're suffering.

At first it just hurts. You get caught in it like an animal in a trap. All you know is that you want it to stop. Then you feel like you've got to get away. The problem being, if the suffering is in you, where is there to go? Get away? To where, to what?

That's when life steps in, if you're lucky and just a little wise. That is, if you haven't yet chained yourself to suffering's dungeon wall. You see, suffering is life's tool of last resort. It's a wake up call; an attempt to bring you to your senses. It's like fear. It arises to get your attention. You've been sleep-walking. "HEY! (With a slap upside your head for emphasis) WAKE UP!" That's all that suffering is for. Don't waste your time blaming or regretting or feeling hard done by. Just wake up. Then do whatever it takes to stay awake and centered. Fear and suffering will eventually sap your energy. They'll wear you down. Resorting to alcohol or drugs will just put you back to sleep. All of them will make you sick. Sickness then takes your suffering to a whole new level. Trust me. You don't want to end up *there* if you can help it. Even then, if it finally wakes you up, life's purposes will be served.

Remember - *IT'S NOT PERSONAL* - even when it feels like it is. Always remembering that one thing has helped me tremendously.

74.

Bad Connections

One of the most beautiful gifts of Tai Chi Qigong is it's gentle progression. In the beginning you find you're just trying to stay soft, trying to relax into your practice. For a half an hour you practice finding tension in the body and letting go of it. In the process you're developing a powerful relaxation response to tension.

Qigong slowly unveils your true nature. Over time you become more of a witnessing presence watching conditioned responses in the body play themselves out.

You begin to unravel. The knots begin to loosen. The life force energy that was captured and held to add fuel to the fire of the stimulus-reaction response re-joins the general circulation. When someone pushes one of your hot buttons you'll find it less and less hot. Eventually there will no longer be any energy available to that particular circuit. You'll feel the "click" but instead of reacting you simply respond by relaxing and dissipating the tension. You watch it trying to load the spring, setting the trap. Seeing it for what it is, you're not so easily caught. Each time you breathe, relax, watch the response – breathe, relax, watch the response; you are exhibiting your level of mastery. You are no longer the conditioned response. In reality, you never were. You have become the watcher. The conditioned behavior can only continue in the dark of unconsciousness.

Qigong dissolves the faulty connections and short circuits in your wiring. It also increases your energetic capacity by unleashing tied up Qi. You become wiser and stronger every time you practice. In time you will begin to recognize more and more places where energy is stuck. You use your greater capacity to strengthen your intent to free further constrictions. You discover that there is no one way that you are, that there are no others doing things to you, making you feel this way and that. It's all internal energy patterns. You practice watching them arise, seeing them for what they are. Cut off their energy, they'll die, and your true nature will, in turn, become more pronounced. You'll feel more alive.

The truth is, you are not what you think. All those reaction-response patterns are a set-up. It's how this organism is programmed. It's mechanical. As you begin to see how robotic you are, you are less and less a robot. Once you wake up to the "I am" without adding anything to it, you are awareness itself. You are that which sees through the illusion of the elaborate construction of "me" stuff. You shine the light of truth on so many things you thought were real and watch as they dissolve into nothing, and the truth of your own revelation sets you free. This is the message of every great tradition however muddled and confused it has become through time.

There have always been subtle hints pointing to the perils of our over-active imagination. Whose childhood was ever free from imagined horrors and fears; monsters lurking under the bed, in the closet, going "bump" in the night? Our ability to create is indeed a double edged sword. Thoughts become things. Be aware. Practice vigilance. Become skilled at shining light into your own dark corners, upon your own false constructions. It isn't a monster that you war against. It is your own imagined self. Be gentle. Be kind.

You are a rhythm and flow of energy. Use it to create a flow of light. Shine it upon the imagined gremlins of life born in thought alone and watch them disappear one by one. Like the concept of evil, they do not exist in the world. They only exist as unconsciousness in you.

75.

Negativity is Contagious

I'm not out to save the world. It doesn't need saving. It's fine just the way it is, just like you. I'm just a guy who got really tired of suffering; tired enough to finally *do* something about it. Every time I find myself moving toward a bad mood, or sadness or cynicism I don't ask myself why, I ask myself how. How is this happening? What's the set-up? What was it that triggered the up-welling feeling? It's always the same culprit: thoughts (more accurately, a whole slough of thoughts) that have gone unchallenged for far too long. In tracing them back to their source, I often find that they were not all born in me, but often came from someone else. I learned them. They're not very original. They're group thoughts, plague thoughts. We catch them from other people.

The downside of being such a social creature is that we are constantly bombarded with the thoughts (and emotions) of others. I suspect that the reason so many revered old masters had the habit of wandering off alone was to give themselves an opportunity to be free of the influences emanating from their fellow humans. We just love to commiserate. Negativity is contagious. It spreads like wildfire.

Having the proper human influence in the form of a mentor or teacher, can be a huge asset, but to find such a one is a rare thing. I've never heard anyone declare "...so there I was in the middle of this ... huge crowd/party/congregation... and this profound clarity suddenly came over me." It's always in the solitude of the mountain cave, desert or wilderness that the seers and sages of mankind have had their revelations. It is in solitude that pure awareness (often referred to as G-O-D) arises.

Being beyond the influence of everyone else's two cents is a prerequisite for the emergence of truth. You see, the truth is always present, it just cannot be discerned amidst the chaos of emotionally charged thoughts and experiences. The truth is that subtle and silent backdrop from which thoughts arise. It's the root of the saying "You can't see the forest for the trees. It's what everything that happens really is.

Once identifying with thoughts and emotions enters the picture, everything becomes so muddied, so quickly, clarity is simply impossible. The agitated ego-mind stirs up either/or thinking, identifies itself with this or that, and then defends its arbitrary position with a tenacity that's often downright frightening, or better yet, it creates an inviolable "me and *my* opinions" out of it all – Good Luck with that one! Whenever you become your emotionally charged thoughts, you are not only declaring war on life, you may be cementing into place a reactionary pattern that will stand for years, if not a lifetime.

Resolve to work a little every day, encouraging through your intent, a restoration of the flow of Qi that has become isolated in an energetic backwater, holding open the floodgate to negative associations in your awareness. Return it to the general circulation and as a result, the floodgate closes. This is accomplished through using your body and breath to create an inner softness that sweeps Qi powerfully along breaking up the energetic log-jams that are required to maintain negative influences of any kind. Once the tension-trapped Qi is drawn naturally away into the ever-strengthening current, obscuring manifestations born of past experience dissolve lifelessly away. Thank God!

76.

On Irritation

It has been said that no enemy can do a man more harm than his own thoughts unguarded - sound wisdom. Negative or worrisome thoughts are exceptionally prolific. Negative thoughts, like most people, are rarely alone. They're like Army ants on the move. One ant - no problem - an irritated flick of the finger to that little scout and Oh, Oh, now you've done it. An alarm goes off and a whole stream of irritated ants answer the call. Whatever was going on a moment before matters little, now it's all about ants. An entire army of the little buggers tumbling over each other to get to you. And to make matters worse, you know the whole fiasco is your fault. Of all the things you could have focused your attention on you had to pick that ant. In no time at all you're in a nightmare of your own creation.

It's as if you Googled something simple like Love or Money and all of a sudden there are 3,293,421 matches flashing sequentially at the speed of thought (modern science says $1/10,000^{th}$ of a second) into your awareness. That's way too fast to make any mental sense, so all those files together create an overwhelming feeling instead. You immediately begin to experience a feeling of irritation about Love or Money and you don't even know why. You can't. This is what we refer to as a mood. 3,293,421 little nibblers are having you for lunch! Trying to change your feelings about Love or Money isn't going to get rid of them. Affirmations and the power of positive thinking aren't going to make them go away. Psychotherapy is not going to work either. You know what will work? Relax, Breathe, Feel - No labels - soft focus, nothing more or less important than anything else. Don't *do* anything. Relax. Breathe. Stay with what is happening. Money is there or it's not. Love is there or it's not. They come, they go. What else do you need to know? Don't look to your computer for answers. 3,293,421 references won't help you resolve anything, but they just may keep you up all night. Don't let irritation get the better of you. Don't flick any ants. Relax. Acknowledge them, watch them, and leave them alone. That is enough.

77.

Through The Back Door

Tai Chi Qigong is about becoming skilled in your awareness of tension. Physical tension is necessary for movement of the body. Proper alignment, muscle tone, posture and coordination, allow us to accomplish maximum physical efficiency with minimum effort. It also greatly reduces the potential for physical injury. The most accomplished physical athletes make their skill look effortless. That kind of proficiency is gained only through practice.

One of the easiest ways to enhance physical ability is through the breath. There is a direct correlation between relaxed, efficient breathing, and physical performance. Holding or halting the breath by and large, have a negative effect on physical effort. Powerful exhalation can serve to enhance physical effort when properly timed. Powerful inhalation focuses mental energy. It is free-flowing, relaxed belly breathing that is most desirable as the norm. As breath flows Qi flows.

Mental states take their cues from both the physical condition and breathing. Mental/emotional relationships are so inextricably linked as to be almost a single entity. They are also directly responsive to breath and body states. This natural response is how we gain mastery of our inner condition. By using physical tension/relaxation, through body and breath, we come in through the back door, so to speak, and use the breath and physical relaxation to influence the mental/emotional component of our nature instead of it happening the other way around. We subtly use to our advantage, a relationship that already exists.

Irregular halted breathing supports mental\emotional agitation. Relaxed belly-breathing supports mental\emotional stability. An automatic response, with just a little practice, becomes a tool of choice. You get to choose the state you wish to support

Whenever you're anxious, excited, or fearful there is a shift in bodily functions. This is how a polygraph (lie detector) works. It registers the shift in bodily function caused by a mental/emotional stressor by measuring heartbeat, breath and in some cases galvanic skin response (which is the chemical marker for the shift). Your response to perceived threats (which in modern humans includes threats to the ego) is ancient; it's part of the reason we're still here. However, most perceived threats in modern society are not physical. They're of the ego variety. Egos interacting with other egos, vying for power and influence, are the hallmark of most human interactions in modern America.

It's the mentality of the pack. It's one more reason that the old Taoist masters had so little tolerance for social convention and class. It's all an artifice. Stuff piled on Self. Making the internal adjustments required as you become increasingly aware of the friction between your true nature and the rules and laws of social interaction (not to mention the price to be paid for breaking them) is not an easy task. To accomplish this you must undertake a system of self-cultivation that short circuits or at least sheds significant light upon your cultural conditioning.

Qigong is such a system. Its methods are simple and reliable. We use body, breath and mind to reverse the conditioning. We don't cultivate radical opinions, become political rebels, or demonize the world. We relax, breathe and move with softly focused attention and bring about a more natural way of functioning utilizing the same methods as our creator, only in reverse. It works either way.

As your subtle senses are honed through continued practice, life becomes a deeper richer experience. You begin to see more clearly how internal processes have constructed, experience by experience, not only a 'you' but also the 'world.' This is how we learn to be in the world but not of it. Awakening to this simple fact is a sure sign of the maturing of your practice. You have not only optimized your physical and mental/emotional functioning, you have brought about, almost incidentally, an awareness of spirit; a realization of the true role of your attention and awareness. It isn't something that you have as an attribute or a sixth sense. It is essentially what you are. It is your "original face, before you were born." Awareness isn't born, it doesn't die. It simply is - omnipresent, omniscient, and omnipotent. And yes, you can get there from here. You become adept through practice. Relax, breathe, move, watch and feel.

78.

Freedom - It's Closer than You Think

You and I have been given the greatest of all gifts. We did nothing to deserve it. It is ours by grace - The gift of life.

By some miraculous coincidence so far beyond the laws of chance or circumstances we are here. Like that which created us, we in turn create. The world in which we exist, the meaning we give it all, the feelings those meanings cause to arise in us – we are creating all of it. It may not feel that way. Sometimes it might feel more like a game of Dodge Ball. It may feel like being trapped, caught in something beyond our understanding and control. It totally depends on who (or what) you think that "you" is. So, it comes down to what you think. So what do you think? Are new and wonderful thoughts endlessly delighting you? Are you so captivated by every moment bringing you something you've never seen before, that every day is an adventure? That's what's happening you know. If we don't see it, it's because something else is in the way. What is it? How did it get there? Investigate.

Life is energy. It flows uniquely through all of the subtle nooks and crannies of this tumble of stuff that we've created. Someone hurt you long ago and the hurt is still there, a boulder in your energy pattern. Someone left or died and there's still a hole in you where the experience of them once was. There's an energy whirlpool there spinning around that empty center. More and more stuff gathers and spins as a result. Countless rockslides of perceived failures, regrets, and self-recriminations come clattering down into your life stream and soon there is hardly a stream at all. The flow is reduced to a meandering trickle through all the clutter. That's where the feeling of being trapped comes from.

The beauty is, it's only a clutter of thoughts, beliefs, and feelings. It's not made of stone. It has no real weight. It all floats effortlessly away if you can just stop devoting so much energy and effort to holding it all in place.

There's nothing to be gained by "keeping it all together". Let it go. It is a quirk of human nature that we often prefer a problem that is familiar to a solution that is not. Let go. You're not going to fall. It may feel like falling, but it's so very different without the fear. Suddenly there's just so much space and so little resistance. Let go.

Freedom is nothing more than that. Free is what you were when the life energy in you was unobstructed. Can you remember?

Get out of your head. Relax, breathe, feel, a little every day gets it done.

"There are thousands of things in the way," you say.

Yes, but you may not be a thousand days from freedom. Every scrap of clutter you remove strengthens the flow. The trickles become floods and floods wash away everything in their path.

79.

Ride the Wave

There was a time in our world where the likelihood of meeting (let alone studying with) a gifted spiritual teacher was extremely remote. In today's world, at least in most industrialized nations, your chances are much improved. Of course the essential questions still remain. Who is authentic? Who truly has something of worth to share? I have been blessed by being a lover of books. Some of the greatest discoveries of my life have been made there, in books. Whenever a voice came to me in the form of the written word, a voice I found clear and true, I would eventually be moved to be with that voice in the flesh, the natural exception being those who were dead. Watch out for that one. Whatever those shining few embodied and shared while alive is usually a real mess within a remarkably short period of time after their passing.

One need only look to the disarray of great faiths of the world; each and every one of them fractured and torn and pasted willy-nilly back together again. The founder of each wouldn't recognize any of them as being what they originally taught. I have to admire the tenacity of the purveyors of religiosity, but I do not – cannot - trust it.

So it is to those whose books I have read and into whose eyes I can look that I restrict my spiritual inquiries. I simply put myself, baggage and all, in their presence and see what happens.

Most espouse their tradition, their lineage, or dead teacher. A few radically oppose the same. It is the ones who have abruptly, usually from some "dark night of the soul" experience, awakened, or dissolved, or collapsed, from what they thought they were that interest me the most. I love the fact they never saw it coming. I find that easy to trust.

That's life in a nutshell isn't it? One day it's this, the next it's that, out with the old, in with the new. Every breath is like that. If you're determined, every thought, every experience, can be like that. Learn to ride the wave. Let it happen. Truly, all that is necessary is to stop resisting it. Quit wearing yourself out trying to somehow stop it. Quit wishing it could be different. It *will* be different. Let it.

80.

The Recognition of Innocence

There are very few people in the world that can remain unaffected by the presence of a child. A part of our nature recognizes the state of innocence that once was ours. The reality is that it is still ours. Life energy unfolding and expressing here and now is what you are. The rest is just a story.

The joy one feels in looking into eyes that reflect that quality in you is what you're seeing. When you look into the eyes of anyone over two or three years old you're no longer seeing a reflection, but a reaction. Something's changed. There's a "me" under construction and your looking becomes a part of that. You are now a witness to the upstaging of innocence by ego; by the edifice of self.

Our relationships from that point on rely for the most part upon a recognition of similar construction styles in another and delighting in momentarily finding an 'other' who is so much like you. You both like Chinese food, love to read, watch sports, etc. You see the world as having certain attributes and look to others for confirmations of your view. Likewise, we can't stand (in relationship), those others that are obviously *so* different. What's *wrong* with them?!

It has been said that the great way is not difficult for those who have no preferences. The wise Seng T'san also said that we shouldn't seek for the truth, only cease to cherish opinions. The result of both is a return to innocence. It is still there. There's a great big pile of stuff on it to be sure, but it's still there.

That discovery lies at the heart of every story of loss and redemption. It is the Golden Fleece of every hero's quest. All of our trials leading us to one undeniable conclusion – Life is not what it was thought to be. Our hero ventures forth from his hobbit hole, or safe harbor on the sea, and finds himself at the heart of a great adventure.

It entails facing the unknown with courage, undaunted by joy or sorrow, success or failure. In the end, our hero is always transformed. What was before seems like a dream. What is now, the new reality. A deep knowing has dissolved the past. The trial by fire has burned the old edifice to nothing, and the phoenix rises revitalized and fully alive from the ashes.

There is a great faith of the world that emphasizes forgiveness. The value of forgiveness is the realization of innocence in the world, in us. If there is guilt in you it is not your guilt. If there is shame in you it's not your shame. All the while, you were mistaken. Forgive yourself. You weren't seeing clearly. How could you? There was so much stuff in the way; from people you were afraid would not love you if your world differed too much from theirs, to who you thought you were according to the story you were told. The story you called yourself.

It was just a story. Close the book. Reality awaits - magically unfolding moment by moment fresh and new, just like you.

81.

Open Heart, Open Mind

The relationship between emotional and physical tension is the most natural thing in the world. Our emotional responses to life experiences get translated into physical responses that literally set the stage for our course of action.

One of the very useful skills that Qigong hones to a fine edge is the ability to break the connection between the emotionally charged (automatic) reaction to a given experience and allow other possibilities.

As I've mentioned, I have a fear of heights. Imagine my surprise when I recently climbed onto a roof in the rain and found that by simply breathing (in 2-3-4, out 2-3-4) the usually paralyzing fear simply could not take hold. In addition, the dizziness and sick feeling that such heights usually induce ceased to materialize. I'm not exaggerating when I tell students Qigong can be practiced anyplace, any time. The rainy roof technique is proof of that. Getting onto the ladder on the way down was still a heart-pounding experience but there was no fear. It's good to have a healthy response to high places. I think I now understand the "thrill" my rock-climbing friends talk about. Thrill feels like fear with a subtle difference. Fear is a reaction. A thrill is a response. Fear is felt in the belly; a thrill in the heart. A heart-felt response is always life affirming. If you "think" you're afraid, you're not. That's apprehension – thinking with the heart.

Did you know that somewhere around half of all of the cells in your heart are neurons? Neurons are the cells your brain is made of. Amazing! Somehow we all know this. How many times have you heard, "Listen to your heart" when counseled by a loving friend? Heart-knowing is a skill that is developed once fear is challenged and displaced.

There is a subtle attribute of balanced Qi that can only be described as a feeling of well-being. It's the truth of things. The nagging feeling that something is wrong with the world is fear in disguise. The heart knows that the world is fine, just as it is. Coming to terms with that or not, determines the quality of this journey each one of us is on. The heart embraces. Fear denies. Love is wholeness. Fear is separation. Either condition is internal. Like any internal art, Qigong is an exercise in discernment. An emotionally muddled point of view is at best unreliable, at worst unbearable. As far as life's purposes are concerned, an open heart reflects an open mind. Open and allow – that is the Qigong way.

82.

Are You a Piano in a Marching Band?

Like the wide and varied instruments of a symphony orchestra, or a marching band, each of us contributes to the symphony of creation. We are tubas and flutes, pianos and triangles, kettle drums and piccolos; each one of us contributing our own qualities and tones, our harmonious or dissonant notes to rhythms and pulses of life.

How well do you know your instrument? What is its range? Is it in tune with other instruments of its kind? Are you a piano in a marching band, a tuba in a string quartet? Sometimes it certainly feels that way.

Aside from simply caring for our instrument we have to practice playing it. A certain physical dexterity is required before you will be able to play the tune you want to play. You'll also have to be able to hear the music in your head before you can feel it in your heart. Know that there are songs in the world you have never heard. Know too that there are songs in you, the world has never heard. It goes both ways.

Practice listening first, so that when you decide to play the harmony is there. Then practice the movements that will be required to play your part well, in the song of the world. Play for the world what you hear inside. If it's beautiful other musicians will be moved to play your song and you theirs. It's going to happen just that way whether you want it to or not.

Henry David Thoreau said it best in *Walden*:

> *If a man does not keep pace with his companions, perhaps it is because he hears a different drummer. Let him step to the music which he hears, however measured or far away.*

It is your destiny to contribute to the symphony of life in a way that is uniquely your own. It is best not to revel in your uniqueness or deny it. Simply learn to let it be, without apology or defense.

Do not waste a single moment bemoaning that because you were born a piano you will never march in the band. Simply explore what you are. You will be delighted when you discover that every note that can be played is what you are. Ten notes at once is what you're capable of. That is your gift. If you find you are a tuba, it is a fine thing to love the sweet trill of a piccolo or the melancholy ache of a weeping violin, but then let your own great booming blasts fill the air and send a thrill through the chorus of which you are a part.

Each and every instrument adds a depth and tone to life's song that would not be there without it. Care for your instrument. Then, practice, practice, practice, and your song will be a source of beauty and joy to others, as well as an affirmation of your own, perfectly expressed through your mastery of the instrument you are.

83.

The Shining

All of the mystical traditions of the world make the effort to clarify the spiritual aspect of life in much the same way. It doesn't matter whether we are talking about the Gnostics of Christianity, the Sufis of Islam, the Zen monks of Buddhism, or the Hindu Sadhus. They all espouse an inner experience of the "truth" that words cannot convey. Yet the signposts of each of them are remarkably similar. An ephemeral "something" that is a "nothing" in the world of conceptual thought. A stillness in which everything moves; a creative intelligence that magically transforms emptiness into manifest form; a shining that finds its way into the physical world of humankind, as well as all of creation.

    The mistake that is generally predominant is to think that these mystics and sages were somehow exceptional beings, "with powers far beyond those of mortal men". That's a story we tell ourselves. They were just like you and I. Each and every one of them was a son or daughter of God, just like you and I. Each and every one of them came to their revelation the same way. They quit believing the story of who and what they were. They took that shining awareness home with them. They quit looking for it. They saw through the silly little edifice of "me". That patchwork of memories, dreams and reflections pasted together to fit what they were taught and told about what was real and what was not. They each realized nothing. They came to understand nothing. They became that without a second, and that changed everything in the world and nothing all at once. What did they gain? Nothing. Here's the kicker –

        "Nothing does not exist."

Don't think about that. Just sit with it. See how it feels. Take deep breaths – relax. Try not to try. See, if you can, the stillness in which the thinking mind moves. Sense if you can, the space which allows this book in your hands to be. That spaciousness is the foundation upon, and within which all reality rests, the seeing of it, the revelation. You now know the truth.

Congratulations!

84.

Old Solomon Was Mistaken

The big bang didn't happen 14 billion years ago. It happened just now. Did you feel it? Wait ....there it is again! Nothing just became something. BANG! Wow. That never happened before, not the way it just happened. That was a first. It's always a first. I'm sorry, but wise Old Solomon was mistaken when he said, "What was once shall be again, and there is nothing new under the sun." Every moment is new, every breath. If you don't believe me, try holding on to the last one… See what I mean?

I used to fret over the cycles of life. I'd be up I'd be down, feeling happy/sad, enlightened/burdened.

"What's wrong with me?" I'd ask. "Why can't I be peaceful? Why can't I be happy? How come every time I think I've got "it" I lose "it"?

One day it just hit me – there is no "it"! "It" is a trick of the mind. "It" is everything all at once. "It" is nothing at all. "It" is not something to get. "It" is what I am. How could I ever lose it? "It" is absurd – utter foolishness. A figment of my imagination.

When the great 20th century sage, Ramana Maharshi was sick with cancer his students and disciples begged him to heal himself. Then one student asked him:

"Where will you go when you die?"

He replied, "Where would I go? I am here."

85.

Nature Always Wins

I recently saw an image of our Sun's magnetic field taken from a satellite: Countless loops of energy, some flowing outward, others gracefully curling back, a dance of circular pathways in ebb and flow.

There was also a magnetic image of the earth taken by that same satellite. What a mess! The energy waves looked like a backlash in a fishing reel, a hopeless tangle of electromagnetic frenzy; a virtual rat's nest devoid of beauty or symmetry. Surely there must have been once, before power plants and appliances and TVs, radios, satellites and cell phones.

That there will be a return to a more natural configuration is inevitable. How will the balance be restored is the question. Rampant technology has changed so many natural energy patterns in our world. What a chaotic effect those changes are having in the matrix of our lovely little planet.

For millions of years, the evolution of life on planet earth has been governed by the dance of the naturally occurring forces of the cosmos with the creative processes of the earth itself. The subtle energies are always the precursors to the more dramatic (violent) ones. Those subtle energies (such as Qi) move in accordance with a creative intelligence, as yet, beyond our understanding. The subtle relationships required for life itself continue to elude us, but one thing is certain. Nature always wins. One way or another, balance is *always* restored.

It is not far fetched to assume that a cooperative effort of restoring any energetic movement to a state of balance would be in alignment with life's purposes. It's true that ultimately chaos is the matrix from which new creations arise. Unfortunately, already established forms reliant on the subtle balance of natural forces never emerge unscathed from such turmoil (if they emerge from it at all).

Crisis is a powerful catalyst for change, but is it necessary? Can balance be restored through our intent? Can we influence the life force that created us? I think we can, if we are in accord with it. We're already connected. It flows through us. The challenge is to serve it through greater awareness. To war with it is sheer folly. A war against ourselves is a battle which can have only one outcome.

I can't help but wonder if that hopeless tangle of the Earth's magnetic field is playing a role in the chaos and confusion present in the hearts of so many these days. What goes around comes around we say, but we're not acting as if we believe it. What can it hurt if we at least try? Balance *will* be restored with or without our cooperation. We certainly have nothing to lose by spending a little time and energy restoring the balance within.

As above, so below, as within, so without - so the ancient edict goes. In embracing our ability to contribute to life's unfolding processes we acknowledge and accept our responsibility to creation itself. Our long sought salvation, as well as self-preservation depends on it. Chaos is a fine starting point, but we've come too far for it to hold sway now. There is a failure of purpose in it. It's an indication that a collapse is in the offing. It needn't be so.

The kingdom of creation operates as powerfully within each one of us, as it does above and below us. Our lives are its tools of transformation; our consciousness, evidence of the universe waking up to itself. You and I play a deep and vital role in that process of awakening. Open to that possibility and it becomes reality. It's what we're here to do. I'm sure of it; as sure as I'm alive.

86.

All Hail Bread and Circuses!

There is significant evidence that what we refer to as civilization has been around a helluva lot longer than 5,000 years. When I look at those depictions of ancient Sumerians in their ornate robes, carefully coiffed hair, and outrageously curled beards I get the distinct feeling they didn't just suddenly wander in from the desert dressed for the Prom.

The body of the sphinx in Egypt is badly eroded by water in a land that has been arid for seven thousand years. Anyone with eyes to see notices how disproportionate the head is to the lion's body on which it is perched. It seems pretty clear that it was a later addition to an already existing monument. How long would it take to design and carve that great lion? How complex a culture would be necessary to envision and then execute such a massive undertaking?

Throughout the world there are gigantic monolithic structures that were old when ancient civilizations discovered them. It would be downright silly to ask, "If they were so advanced, where's the evidence of their TVs, microwaves, and cell phones?" So we write them off as 'Stone Age' and get on with scientific progress and economic growth.

Perhaps the greatest legacy the Darwinian model of evolution has left us with is the tendency to automatically associate *old* with primitive and *new* with advanced. How perfectly such hubris would suit our picture of our wonderfully modern, and technologically sophisticated, selves. I ask you, what have we built that will still be standing in 5,000 years?

One has only to read a single book like Graham Hancock's *Fingerprints of the Gods* to seriously question conventional history's account of what has been. As for the whole extraterrestrial thing, are our imaginations so limited that we would rather attribute ancient technologies and stories of giants and magnificent beings to travelers from outer space than our own dear ancestors? Who can even imagine the countless travails that this earth of ours has been through throughout the vast epochs of time? How many times has man risen to incredible heights and been knocked flat by asteroids, comets, and supernovas from space? How many times has the earth shrugged and heaved from within and created worldwide conditions hostile beyond imagining to all life upon it?

Only stories and stones remain. Nature's processes claim everything else in time.

What intrigues me is what were those other civilizations doing in their time? Where's their garbage? What did *they* think was important? What did they know that we have yet to imagine? Who can say?

The fickle priorities of culture have insidious ways of perpetuating themselves. What has the goal of owning a car that will rust into the ground and uses the goo of life long dead for power, while living in air-conditioned comfort got to do with the greater scheme of things? I guess we'll see. What is the cost of believing that all roads lead to Rome? It can only be that Rome is where we'll end up. All hail bread and circuses!

87.

Quantum Weirdness

Here in the 21st century there is nothing quite as exciting to me as the current explorations in Quantum physics. For the first time in modern history, we have scientific model of what the ancient shamans, seers, and sages have been saying all along. We're all connected, but it's not just us – everything's connected to everything else.

The mind boggles at the thought. It will tell you incessantly that everything is clearly separate from everything else. Yet time and again in this strange and wonderful realm of Quarks and Neutrinos and the influence of Charm (this is science mind you), all that the mind would tell us is impossible is proved to be unquestionably evident, in experiment, after experiment.

Things *can* be in two places at once. Time exists only as a concept in the mind. At the heart of matter there is no matter at all, just what Einstein derisively termed "Quantum weirdness". Sometimes this weirdness acts like a particle. Sometimes it acts like a wave. It can blink in and out of existence. Sometimes it appears, then disappears then appears again somewhere else without going through any space! Sometimes it communicates to a twin particle across vast distances taking absolutely no time to do so. It's instantaneous.

There is even a distinct possibility that we oscillate between multiple universes which each contain certain possibilities and outcomes that come into play depending on what we believe is possible and what we believe is not. That we see only what we want to see and call our seeing proof! More than anything else, we may resemble a television tuner that is constantly flipping channels as we hopelessly try to construct that craziness into a story that makes some kind of sense. The power of the human imagination unleashed upon creation - pretty amazing stuff. What will happen when we learn to let go of how we think of ourselves and the world around us?

How will this experience of life unfold when such outrageous possibilities are consciously embraced and cooperated with? When we learn to acknowledge that we exist on the cutting edge of creation there will be miracles unfolding upon miracles (as if it's ever been anything else). That excites the hell out of me. How about you?

88.

Skin to Skin, Heart to Heart

How we begin our lives has more to do with how we live them than anyone ever dreamed. In the first few hours, days, and weeks a newborn's internal processes are very unstable. All of the time you spent in the womb you were surrounded by the rhythms and pulses of your mother. One of the more surprising findings of modern science is that the mother-child relationship during breastfeeding has as much to do with stabilizing the internal vital rhythms of life, as it does with physical nourishment. For nine months the rhythms and flows of the baby are supported by those of the mother. Then quite suddenly, you found yourself a separated, independent system. It took a while for your vital functions to self-regulate. Nature wisely integrated stabilizing your internal rhythms with being fed at your mother's breast.

The mother holds her child skin-to-skin, heart-to-heart while breastfeeding. This intimate proximity is so much more than just soothing and familiar. The heartbeat, breath and voice of the mother are a continuation of the womb experience. There is an actual harmonizing, an entrainment, of the newborn's rhythms with those of the mother. Every feeding, your heart literally communed with the heart of your mother. It has also been revealed that newborns do not have poor vision as was believed for so long, but see faces clearly at 10-18 inches. Again the perfect proximity of mother while at the breast helped your little brain to begin organizing and recognizing what your senses were telling you of the world. From our first breath, feeling nurtured and cared for is vital for every one of us.

As we mature into fully independent and more autonomous beings, that initial process continues. Nature finds what works and sticks with it. We resonate with others (or not) as a result of our ongoing emotional experiences, sensing pleasant, (supportive) or unpleasant. We all struggle to somehow resonate with the world; to harmonize with it; to feel at home in it. The essential problem is what it's always been – we do not live in the world, the world lives in us.

Our internal rhythms, from the very beginning, determined our experience. Unstable rhythms create chaotic, anxious, experience. So how do we stabilize them at this stage of the game? To what nurturing support do we turn to adjust ourselves? The rhythm most fundamental to our independent existence is, and always has been, the breath. The closest we will ever come to returning to that initial nurturing support provided upon our arrival is that precious gift, of life on our own - Our breath.

Embrace it. Experiment with it. Become deeply intimate with it. It is your touchstone to perception. Use it; inhale – 2-3-4, exhale 2-3-4, six times is good. Ten times is better. A little self-talk helps things along. Repeat to yourself, "With each exhalation comes deeper and deeper relaxation." Feel your body relax and soften.

Breathe through the nose … smooth, fine, deep and even. It will soothe your hurts. It will quiet your fears. It will bring you peace. It is your mother now, feeding you.

89.

It is what it is

Your greatness is determined by all of the things you embody, and in so doing become. Your diminishment rests upon the limitations that you accept and then cease to question. Definitions obscure reality. We think by defining ourselves in the world we come to know who we are. There is more often than not, a subtle self-deceit at work in that attitude. The reality is there is nothing that you are not.

You are cruel and you are kind. You are masculine and feminine. You are a speck of life in a vast universe and the very center of the whole magnificent play as well. To learn to rest easily in such an outrageous situation is our challenge; to remain poised and balanced as Yin and Yang relentlessly exert themselves. In endless tension the process continues, each aspect begging us to add strength and life to its continued existence.

There is nothing you are supposed to be. You cannot fail. You are creation's wonderful experiment in possibility. You are a work in progress. Whatever you choose to give your attention to is inexorably brought to life by that attention. How powerful you are! How mysterious your creation.

I give my attention to thoughts and feelings arising from within, pick up a pen, make some squiggles and here they are in your hands. Am "I" here in your hands? I assure you I am not. As I squiggle can those around me hear anything? As you read this, can you? Whose voice is it that you hear? Mine? Yours? Whose? What's going on?

Awareness is going on. Awareness is playing with itself (If it had a mother, she'd be having fits!) and having a ball. "Where is it? Show it to me!" the mind demands. Can you see how silly that is? How can it ever be what you think?

How perfect the very first line of the *Tao Te Ching* is: "*The Tao that can be told is not the true Tao.*" The word Tao (pronounced dow) means simply the way.

Some say it is the way to live. Some say it is the way to true understanding; I feel it is creation's infallible compass eternally pointing to the unbroken wholeness that underlies the emergence any action, function, thought, or thing. It is the way of the one as many. It is in the end, a way of seeing, hearing, acting, and being in the world; a way of perceiving the root or heart of a thing; of recognizing the process of creation in all of its guises. It's not an idea, religion or philosophy. It includes everything. It opposes nothing. It is what it is. How perfect.

90.

Synchronicity

One of the great 20th century explorers of the mental/emotional realm of human experience was C.G. Jung. It was he who first referred to the strange little coincidences that arise from time to time in our lives as synchronicities. A synchronicity is when you think of calling a friend you haven't talked to in a while and they call you, perhaps the same day or even the moment when you have the phone in your hand. Synchronicity is often the crucial catalyst in bringing about a set of circumstances that are often fortuitous, marvelously coincidental, and inevitably unforeseen.

Most recently in our household, my son, Bradley asked my wife and I, about the possibility of getting couch for his room. The very next day my boss casually asked if I knew of anyone who needed a couch. He was moving and was selling one for $300.00. I mentioned that my son needed one but didn't have $300.00, at which point he offered to let it go for less, adding that he would accept installment payments to make it easier on Brad. I was quite tickled at the coincidence and was looking forward to sharing my tale of good fortune with the family that evening.

Upon my arrival home my wife asked if I would help bring in Brad's new couch from our mini-van! She explained how she'd been driving home from a friend's house and noticed a woman putting a "free" sign on a fine looking couch that her boys had just carried out to the side of the road and pulled over. My wife told them her tale, all present chuckling at the way of things and then they proceeded to load it into the van for her which just so happened to have the rear seats removed. Now *that's* synchronicity!

There are whole books about it, one of the best of them written by Jung himself. Synchronicity is one of life's little miracles. I have no doubt you can probably share a few synchronicities of your own. How wonderful when situations or circumstances so far removed from the realm of chance, unfolding effortlessly in response to our wishes and desires. A million to one shot spontaneously occurs in response to our needs, or perhaps it's as subtle as the sudden appearance of an affirmation to an unstated thought; a thought known only to you.

The timing is usually what makes it so undeniably marvelous. Of all the things that could happen, why that? Why now? are often the questions. With the most memorable ones there isn't a question at all. Just a jaw-dropping, awe-struck moment in which we hear the *Twilight Zone* theme.... Do do, do do – Do do, do do start to play in our heads.

The appearance and frequency of synchronicity in your life is a fine way of determining how well your life is working. A fun way of peeking in on the mystery of creation and discovering much to your delight, that it somehow knows you're here. Synchronicity is the outcome of throwing your conscious intent into the mix of polarized possibility and having the weight of it somehow tip the scales your way.

Destiny is not fixed. Possibility outcomes are always subject to revision. See things differently and the things you see will change.

Remember that things are rarely what they seem at first. Look again, and again, and again - Each time with new eyes. It isn't easy, but it is well worth the effort. Clear-seeing unencumbered by thought, is a pearl of great price.

91.

Attention!

Ask someone you know what love is. Ask them what God is. Ask them what the most important thing in life is. Then ask them again in a year or two. I can tell you what you'll learn. You'll learn that no two people will give you the same answer. You'll learn that the answer you get a year or two down life's road won't be the same one you got before. So don't ever settle in to thinking you know someone. You don't. You can't. We're all involved in an endless search for meaning. The meaning of what you ask? Of whatever we're paying attention to. Yes, it's that simple. Your attention is pure gold. Everyone and everything you encounter wants it. Your attention is focused awareness. Awareness is consciousness manifested and everything, EVERYTHING wants to exist. In the subtle realms, as nothing moves inexorably toward becoming something, attention is the nurturing medium in which it happens.

Love, God, greed, resentment, joy, the 10,000 things; all of it must be given our attention to exist. So, what have you been giving your attention to today? What have you made real that could not exist without you? Are you happy with your choices? Did you remember they *were* your choices? Life, deep meaningful life has a cost – You have to pay attention.

Do not spend your treasure frivolously. Be prudent in your choices. Choose wisely to what you give it, and those with whom you share it. Like a master craftsman, bring all your skills to the creations of your life. Half measures won't do. Don't let quiet desperation creep in and undermine your intentions. Be patient with yourself.

There is an old story of a beggar who everyday, sat and begged upon a box he inherited from his father. One day a wandering monk piqued his curiosity when he asked the beggar as he walked by,

"What's in the box?" When the beggar pried it open he found it contained a wondrous treasure. Needless to say, from that moment on, he no longer saw himself as a lowly beggar, but then he never was.

92.

The Mission

There are stories that "Old Timers" love to tell about how different life used to be. They're often very entertaining in the beginning. To hear of life with horses, before there were cars, or life on the farm before rural electrification, brings the past to life again. Just listening to such tales brought to light from the memory of the teller lets us see the world through the eyes of another, and yet there is a certain sadness to it all.

Upon hearing the tale for the tenth or twentieth time I can't help but feel that the teller is caught and contained in the story. The theme of the tale begins to emerge; perhaps of love lost or a time that was somehow better or truer than now. The tale becomes less of this is what happened: and more of "this is who I am." or this is how I became me. They have become the story. The book of their life falls open again and again to that same defining page.

I feel as if I'm looking upon a wild and wondrous creature that has been captured and kept in a cage far too small. A cage of its own making brought into being through a simple act of mistaken identity. A projection of thoughts and feelings registered in a distant time playing out in the now, and yet there is also a certain sweetness to it. We're *so* sentimental. Nature is not. Not one bit.

Life feeds on life. Life must consume to continue on. Sentimentality will not feed you in any beneficial way. Let it go. A healthy compassion is what is called for. A mutual recognition of life's harshness effortlessly creates a common ground of understanding and the necessity of acceptance of what is. To ease another's suffering through recognition of our own is one of our more admirable traits. It makes forgiveness so much easier. What, but forgiveness; of the past;

of the moment; of any perceived hurt, so completely returns us to the wholeness of our humanity? We are not here to fragment ourselves.

There is a wonderful scene in the movie *The Mission* when a character played by Robert DeNiro, who is in training to become a priest, is dragging a net filled with his armor, weapons, and saddle as his self-imposed penance from his past as a slaver. As he struggled through the jungle, you get the sense that he is almost broken by the frustration and exhaustion of literally dragging the weight of his past behind him. It is his self-imposed penance to atone for what he once was. As he climbs a wet and perilous escarpment, one of the warriors waiting near the top recognizes him as the one who had hunted and killed so many from his tribe. Grabbing him by the hair, he moves to slit DeNiro's throat. When DeNiro just closes his eyes and waits for what he feels would be the fitting end to his travail, the warrior asks the priest with him why he does not resist. "He killed his brother" the priest answers. The warrior contemplates this for a moment and then instead of killing him, uses his knife to cut him loose from his burden, and it clatters down the rocky cliff, disappearing into the river below. In spite of all he had done to them their compassion so overwhelmed him, as they helped him to the top, that he broke down and wept at the wonder of it. As he wept, they laughed at him. And weeping, he remembered how someone laughing at him had always made him so angry he could kill, and he too began to laugh. In that moment, it was done. His suffering was over, and you felt his rebirth. I love that scene.

Breaking free of the past is always so sweet. The door to the cage we have made pops open, and we are invited to step out into a world of possibilities for which we are destined and designed.

93.

It Is, and It Is Not

I used to think that enlightenment was a permanent affair. That once the bush started burning, once that outrageously beautiful sunset blasted so powerfully through me that it became impossible for me to drive; it would forever after be there. It is and it is not.

The light of seeing is there. The light of knowing is there, yet it is more or less obscured by my state of mind at any given time. It appears more or less pronounced dependent upon where my attention is. Am I present or lost in thought? To what am I giving my attention? It ebbs and flows like a tide.

I was thinking just a moment ago of a friend now dead. I was questioning whether or not he was really gone. I hadn't seen him in 15 years when he called to tell me he was dying. I called him back a month later and his wife said, "He's gone," yet just a moment ago he made me laugh. I thought of him and I heard his voice and I saw his face and then he laughed, and so did I.

I think enlightenment is like that. It's just waiting to be remembered. It's just waiting for you to turn your attention and see it. Live lightly in your head. See clearly with your heart, and it is there like and old friend – laughing.

94.

Ten Steps To a Better You

We can view our lives from within countless rigid contexts and usually do. We see ourselves first and most powerfully though, in the light of family. Family is the sub-culture that prepares us for the greater cultures of society, religion, state, nation and the world. Our parents are the first Gods of our lives, the first to set the rules by which we will be judged, and judge ourselves. They are the first reflection to which we conform.

How we see ourselves in relation to others is powerfully influenced by whether you're born first or last, male or female, in poverty or prosperity or somewhere in-between. It all will play a part in the unfolding of the "me" you will become. Slaps or smiles at age three will determine your actions at twenty three, more than you'll ever know, and yet the possibility of conscious transformation is always there. None of it is written in stone.

If there's a glitch in the program hitting the delete key won't work. Reading "Ten Steps to a Better You" won't have a chance against that knot in your gut that locks your breath in your throat every time someone yells at you. All you can do is remember to breathe and relax, watch and feel, and then focus your intent upon breaking the energetic connection to that reaction. Then make that response a habit.

Habits work. For us, or against us, the force of habit is undeniable. What we have to work towards (and I won't lie, it *is* work) is creating a response to a reaction. When someone yells (or whatever the trigger might be) the knot in the gut and the halting of the breath WILL occur. The only thing that matters then is what you do from that point on. You are not responsible for your reactions. You are only responsible for how you respond to them.

95.

Life Is a Trickster

One of the greatest gifts Qigong has bestowed upon me is the ability to laugh at myself. I remember the father of an old girlfriend saying "You're too young to be so damn serious, lighten up." I think it was during my Nietsche phase. He's the philosopher that got it all figured out and then killed himself. It just goes to show where a really powerful mind can take you. Life doesn't take itself seriously at all.

When the Pacific cod get together along the coast of North America to spawn, there's so much sperm and roe in the water you can see it from outer space. My Father told me once that to masturbate and then flush semen down the toilet was a sin. The mind reels...

It's *not* personal. Live lightly. Make mistakes. Lots of them! You'll learn a lot. You will be wise beyond your years. Who's born wise? How do you think you get that way?

Life is a trickster. It pretends to be something it's not. So isn't it logical that you're going to have the inclination to be something you're not? It's not your fault. To think it is, is just silly. See it as the silliness it is. Then have a good laugh. The universe has glued a quarter to the sidewalk and is waiting and watching for you to notice. If you see it and try to pick it up, and laugh when you realize what's really going on...YOU WIN!

96.

Holy Fire

All is energy in motion. Your relationship to that which created you is an energetic one. Becoming aware of the subtle bonds of energetic relationship is the way the true context of our life reveals itself.

E-motion colors your experience of the world. When you learn to balance your emotional nature, your experience of the world will, in turn, be more balanced; your point of view more reliable. If your life feels chaotic, changing relationships, your job, where you live, or anything else will not bring you peace. Balancing your emotions will.

So often we hear that it is our thoughts that must be changed. I don't agree, simply because they're not *your* thoughts. They are the thoughts (or more accurately, the level of thought) you are resonating with.

If you are fearful, you are going to have anxious, fearful, thoughts. If you are joyous you will tune in to the joyous level of thought and so on. The tone of your emotion determines the context of your thinking not the other way around. Your thoughts reference your emotional state for validity. What you experience as real or more real than something else is the emotional "memory" that underlies the thought.

Countless times in my life I have tried to change my mind about something with little success. When I looked deeper I found an emotionally charged experience coloring things from the hidden realms of the past. This is why most "thinking" is actually a repetitious and useless experience of acquired "attitude" and not really thinking at all. It is a reflection of polluted inner environment. You've got to clean things up. You don't just throw it out. You can't. You've got to burn it. A "holy fire" is required.

Just as sure as there would be no life on earth without the energy and light of the sun, there will be less life in you until you stoke the embers of your intent and create a fire of transformation within. That's when things really start to change.

You are a wonder of potential transformation. When you realize you are form born of formlessness; when you begin to move in that direction, there are fewer restrictions imposed by form, and freedom from the form your thoughts have taken (or more accurately the level of thought you are resonating with) becomes a real possibility. Thoughts are things. So are emotions. Thoughts are secondary. Feelings are primary. Know that. You are an animal. Animals have feeling. They don't have thoughts. Feelings came first, thoughts – later.

97.

Coincidentia Oppositorum

In Western mythology there is a recurring theme posited by scholars like Joseph Campbell and Daniel Deardorff of coincidentia oppositorum. It is a juncture that reveals and allows the sacred to permeate our lives. That point of tension that exists between the realm of spirit and the world of form.

Coincidentia – co-incident; happening at the same time. Oppositorum – oppositions. It's a crossroads that looks like this: ☯. It can also look like this: †. It is the state of balanced tension in which neither yin nor yang, heaven or earth, form or formlessness dominates. It is a state of balance in which polarized opposites co-exist; a mystical wedding where two become one. A magical moment in which reality shows itself for what it is: an inherent point of possibility; a dynamic tension poised to create.

It is dependent on form, yet is formless. It exists where inner and outer meet. It arises simultaneously from within and without, and strangely enough it often requires a hero's descent into Hades (which interestingly enough means "the invisible") to bring its power back to the world. A power that appears like a flash of lightning in our awareness –Aha! (The 'Holy Instant' of A Course in Miracles).

All of the ancient mythologies are pointing to the recognition of this all-important aspect of our place in creation. Every time we daydream and come back we have been on that journey. Every time a negative emotion wells up and takes us over, we have been snatched from the light, into the dragons' cave. We have fallen down the rabbit hole. We've gone mad for a moment and then been dropped abruptly back into the world of body and senses. Is it any wonder that we find ourselves stumbling like confused sleepwalkers through the world - the dream – and the world again?

The way of Qigong is to learn the skill of embodying the realm of spirit, giving it free reign to come and go as it will. We can know the dream for what it is, and so remain an open conduit, an available instrument through which the powers of heaven can express on Earth. We can learn to call this strange state of affairs home – to be in the world but not of it.

It is the dragon's path appearing and disappearing with every step. It *is* possible to be at home in every moment neither here nor there, recognizing and embracing both at once. The past cannot hold you back. The future pulls you ever so gently forward, not with hope, but with promise. It takes a bit of doing to remain skillfully poised with a foot in both worlds, but it can be done. It just takes a little practice.

98.

It Takes a Warrior's Spirit

I have always admired the great Warriors of history. I wouldn't doubt that it probably had something to do with seeing *Spartacus* as boy. What a hero! A man who's slave army challenged the power of mighty Rome in a time when the Roman Empire relied heavily upon the labor of slaves. Even when his slave revolt was finally put down, and he and his warriors were crucified all along the Appian Way. The aristocracy of Rome still so feared what he stood for that for over a hundred years to even utter his name was against the law.

Then I was inspired to read the writings of the wise and brave, Marcus Antoninus Aurelius, general, philosopher, and the last of the great leaders of the Roman Republic before it began its deplorable decline as Empire. I admired him for being such a keen observer of human nature; so aware of humanity's potential for greatness, as well as our potential for ruin, should we fail to cultivate our highest selves.

In high school, my attention turned to the East. Myamoto Musashi captured my testosterone soaked imagination. He was the most famous of the Master swordsmen of Japan. After killing 32 men in one on one duels (rather like the fabled gunfighters of the old West), challengers finally determined that to challenge him was to die, and left him alone. He then put away his sword and became a poet, and a sculptor, and a painter of sublime sensitivity; the epitome of the honorable Japanese scholar/warrior.

And then home to the West and Crazy Horse, the last of the great Sioux warriors of the American plains. He was known to be fearless in battle. He preferred counting coup (touching your enemy with a stick) to killing. He felt that the cavalry soldiers had no honor, shooting their enemies from so far away. He despised them for killing defenseless women and children. He was the last of the great Sioux war chiefs to surrender. To surrender his freedom, knowing full well he would have to give up living in a sacred way; roaming the Great plains, hunting, communing in solitude with The Great Spirit, following only his self made laws, must have been the hardest thing he ever had to do. It was probably a blessing that in backing away from the stench of the stockade to which they led him, that he was impaled upon a nervous young soldier's prodding bayonet and died the next day.

    As long as I can remember I have had an affinity for the warrior spirit in man. I am entranced by that inherent nobility and valor that inspires certain men to fight for what they know in their heart to be right. I cannot help but admire those courageous souls who affirm through their actions the existence of a higher calling that they honor with their lives; perfectly willing to lay that life down, if that is what's called for. They will engage in battle when they must, but are not fond of it. Like the noble Arjuna, deeply troubled at the prospect of slaying his countrymen upon the battlefield in The Bhagavad Gita, all true heroes have a deep reverence for life. They are those who dedicate themselves body and soul to their principles, to their fellow warriors, to the good. They do not let fear dictate their actions. They have acquired through virtuous action, an inner knowing of who and what they are. They know that living a human life requires a special kind of courage every day, if it is to be lived well.

    A Warrior's spirit is a basic requirement for those who would seek a life of meaning. A warrior's wisdom is required to know when to fight, and when not to, when to rest, when to seek solitude, and come to know and perfect the skills that will be required when we are inevitably called to action. It is such a subtle thing, this infallible knowing of the true source of one's power.

    Yet, how powerfully it resonates with something deep in our nature ~ this irresistible impulse, to have our lives serve some greater purpose. It's as if we almost remember... what we're here to do.

99.

Is It God, or Is It You?

In 1977 I came across a wonderful little book, *Stalking the Wild Pendulum, on the mechanics of consciousness*. It was written by a marvelously creative fellow by the name of Itzhak Bentov, and I knew then, it was one of those books that would change my view of life, God, and the universe, forever.

Mr. Bentov was a mechanical engineer, though he had no formal education. He too was one of my heroes. He referred to himself as a real "Nuts and Bolts" man. He made part of his living as an inventor. One of his inventions that you and I, and children everywhere, should be ever so grateful for, is the painless hypodermic needle.

While working on the problem he kept dreaming of snakes – *poisonous* snakes. He began to have the feeling that the dreams meant something so he focused his efforts in that direction and discovered that the perfect design of the painless hypodermic needle already existed in nature's design of the snake's hollow fang. All he had to do was copy it. A real "nuts and Bolts" guy? – Hardly.

To my mind, Itzhak Bentov was a practicing mystic of the highest order. His wife Mirtala in the Preface of his second book, *A Cosmic Book, on the mechanics of creation* says that he believed that evolution pushes humanity toward Godhood, "Whether we like it or not." I certainly cannot improve on a few more things she had to say about him:

> *Ben liked to tell the story of how, at the age of nine, he began his search for God. Defying his Jewish background, Ben decided to test the existence of God with a ham sandwich, forbidden by his religion. Moreover, he was going to eat it on Yom Kippur, a high Jewish holiday of fasting and atonement. Eating a ham sandwich was bad enough, but on Yom Kippur, what could be more challenging to God?*

So as not to endanger anybody's life (what if his deed caused the roof to collapse?), he went to a city park, sat on a bench, and bit into the sandwich. He looked up: no lightning, no brimstone. Maybe God hadn't noticed? He took another bite. Nothing. He finished his sandwich and concluded that there must be more to God than what he had been told. His life long search had begun.

There was nothing small about Ben. The scope of his quest was: Who are we? Where are we going? What is the nature and structure of reality? What is the purpose of evolution? What is consciousness? He would begin his talks by saying, "Now we will talk about all there is. From atom to cosmos. From humanhood to Godhood. And that's a lot to talk about."

...In his introduction to Stalking The Wild Pendulum he wrote," I do not claim that the information contained here is the final truth, but I hope it will stimulate more thinking and speculation by future scientists and interested laymen."

... Ben was hesitant to reveal this material because of its unusual, personal nature, but finally decided that it might help some other traveler on the way. With that in mind, he began to write down his experiences.

I never met Itzhak Bentov, but his books dramatically influenced my journey of spirit, my thinking, my life. He was one of my very best teachers, and for that, I am forever grateful.

100.

Choose Wisely and Well

The content of your life may be beyond your control, but the context in which you view it is always yours to choose. It is that view, expansive or contracted, that ultimately determines your reality. It is my sincere wish that you choose wisely and well. I leave you with the inspirational words of Dr. David R. Hawkins, M.D., Ph.D., consciousness researcher extraordinaire, and a true 21st century sage:

> *The desire to reach enlightenment is already a divine gift to be treasured and revered. "Many are called but few are chosen" could be rephrased as "Many are called but few choose to follow." Thus the choice is by decision and assent of the inner will, and by this assent, the enormous power of Divine Will aligns with intention and empowers devotion to overcome all obstacles.*

~ Discovery of the Presence of God (p. 45)

* FIN *

Recommended Resources:

Feel free to contact me by Email at babawanjr@hotmail.com

Here are a few of the most effective Qigong sets that I personally practice and teach for the continued potent benefits each imparts…

Justin Stone's Tai Chi Chih, a 20 pattern set is a simple but powerful qigong easily learned by anyone regardless of age or physical condition. Many traditional taiji practices are difficult to learn and take years to master. This is not one of them. It is potent, healing, very meditative, and takes about a half an hour a day to practice. Further information is available at www.taichichih.org.

Steven Ridley's Harmony Qigong, a 23 pattern set is a Step up from TCC. It requires average flexibility and provides physical conditioning as well as tremendous healing potential. Harmony has been my preferred personal daily practice since 2003. It too, takes about a half an hour a day. This is the Qigong that eliminated my migraine headaches. Also recommended: Steven's 'Breathing Methods for Health and Harmony." Contact: stevenridley@comcast.net to order.

18 Forms Qigong, A traditional Chinese Qigong set, is a rigorous and thoroughly enjoyable experience for those who desire a more physically demanding practice that delivers a wide spectrum of benefits for the half an hour a day it requires. Steven Ridley has an excellent manual and DVD available.

Simple Qigong easily learned from a book:

The Swimming Dragon by T.K. Shih - A simple standing qigong using a repeating pattern of great potency.

Beautiful Heart, Beautiful Spirit (Shing-ling-mei) **by Katherine Orr.** A 6 pattern set of Wudang Qigong, thoroughly explained and easily learned from the excellent illustrations.